WHY SELL

LIES

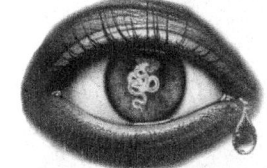 WHEN THE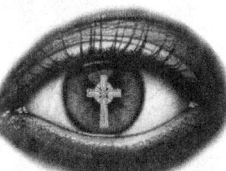

TRUTH

IS

FREE

CARLOS WALLACE

e Order

AN WIPES O
ARMED FORC

Chicago Defender

States' Rights"

Alan Dean: Rising Above Bias

Alan Paul Dean, Sr., was the first African-American officer to serve aboard the USS *Wisconsin* and one of only a few in the Navy during the Korean War.

Born in 1927, Alan Paul Dean spent his childhood growing up in rural Sleepy Hollow, New York, enduring the hardship of Great Depression-era poverty. Dean recalls in his memoirs that the most his carpenter father earned during this time was $13 a week. The grandson of former slaves, Dean said that he would always remember two key lessons his father taught him as a child:

> " *Never use the excuse that you are black as a reason for your failure.*" and " *Growing up poor did not mean you didn't have pride. We were taught to hold our heads up, work hard, and respect everyone in our lives regardless of their station.* "

Cover design by Deonne Moore

Back cover photo by Liz Faublas-Wallace

Interior images by Shelby MacKellar and Cesar Gonzalez

Interior photos by Carlos Wallace

ISBN: 979-8-9889033-4-5
           979-8-9889033-5-2
           979-8-9889033-6-9

Printed in the United States of America

For permissions, inquiries, or other requests, please contact:
Million Dollar Pen, Ink.
84-49 168th Street
Jamaica, New York 11432

Email: editor@MillionDollarPenInk.com
Website: www.MillionDollarPenInk.com

Wallace, Carlos

WHY SELL LIES WHEN THE TRUTH IS FREE

Coming of Age Fiction
Family Drama
Social and Cultural Issues

First Edition: 2024

DISCLAIMER

The views and opinions presented in this work of fiction are exclusively those of the author and do not necessarily reflect the perspectives or beliefs of Million Dollar Pen, Ink. The publisher does not assume responsibility for the thoughts, beliefs, or viewpoints conveyed within the text.

The author assumes full responsibility for the content of this book, including any material that may be considered controversial or sensitive. The publisher neither endorses nor validates the ideas, opinions, or viewpoints expressed by the author.

Readers are strongly encouraged to engage critically and independently with the content of this book, forming their own judgments and interpretations. The publisher does not guarantee the accuracy, completeness, or timeliness of the information presented in this book and shall not be held liable for any consequences resulting from its use or interpretation.

Additionally, any names, characters, or incidents depicted within this book are entirely fictional and are intended solely for the purpose of storytelling. Any resemblance to actual persons, whether living or deceased, or real events is purely coincidental.

Although every effort has been made to ensure the accuracy of the information contained in this book, the publisher makes no representations or warranties of any kind, whether express or implied, regarding the completeness, accuracy, reliability, suitability, or availability of the information, products, services, or related graphics contained within this book.

Under no circumstances shall the publisher be held liable for any loss or damage, including but not limited to indirect or consequential loss or damage, or any loss or damage arising from this book's use.

Any discrepancies or concerns regarding the content of this book should be directed to the author.

Publisher:

Million Dollar Pen, Ink.

DEDICATION

This book is dedicated to two discerning individuals who recognized the potential within me, even when I had yet to see it in myself. Gilbert Pritchett and Jeff Sewell, I owe you both a debt that can never be repaid.

While there are many others to whom I could extend similar appreciation, I must emphasize that, within the context of the artistic journey, these two men especially have had an indelible impact on my life.

As a child, I attended Eastside Elementary in Jacksonville, Texas. I was a reserved, introverted young Black student in Mrs. Hancock's third-grade class. One day, I was summoned to the principal's office, Mr. Wilson. I approached his office cautiously because I had no idea what I had done to earn the worrisome invite! I turned over the day's events in my mind trying to identify which of my actions could be considered troublesome. One thing was certain; no matter what the infraction, this would not sit well with my parents!

I felt the walls of the corridor contract around me as I made my way to his office. I was greeted by a very kind woman who I would come to know as the head of the drama department at Lon Morris College. The school, once accredited, was a venerable two-year institute of higher learning and offered a comprehensive liberal arts and science program. Sandy Duncan, Margo Martindale, and Neal McCoy are among the college's notable alumni. What could this woman possibly want with me?

To my surprise, I was asked to participate in an upcoming theatrical production, in which I would be cast as a young Black boy. Well, I definitely fit that bill!

The proposition caught me off guard, but I responded cautiously that I would need to consult with my mother (an admission that met with a few gentle chuckles). The lady nodded understandably and awaited parental consent (which by the way my mom was happy to give).

Shortly after, I embarked upon my theatrical journey, eager to review the script and prepare for my role.

I was cast as the grandson of a freed slave, a character brought to life by Gilbert Pritchett, affectionately known as Bro. Gil. In this formative experience, he assumed the role of a mentor and imparted valuable acting lessons along the way. At the time, I was not aware of the passion this experience had ignited within me. I eagerly followed instructions, mostly out of respect (and gratitude) for the trust my mother placed in me. Why I was ever selected for the role though, remained a mystery.

The conclusion of this five-day theatrical venture fell on a significant date—Friday, February 15, 1980, which coincided with my ninth birthday. The cast surprised me with a celebration complete with a cake, balloons, and gifts; a joyous occasion any nine-year-old would cherish. Tears welled in my eyes, and I wasn't sure if they were from joy or sadness. I truly enjoyed my party, but this was a reminder we would probably never see one another again.

It would be more than four decades before I would reconnect with Mr. Pritchett. Our reunion proved to be an extraordinary occasion, during which we spent hours reminiscing about that pivotal week. He was also able to shed light on the reason I was cast in the part. He said I possessed an innate quality that showed I was the most suitable candidate for the role.

To this day, I count this as my first official, structured role in a meticulously organized production, and perhaps what inspired me to write, direct, produce, and act in award-winning films.

This surely was an experience that played a pivotal role in awakening my enduring affinity for the arts.

Jeff Sewell. Where do I start?

Jeff entered my life during what I consider to be my third phase of adulthood.

The first encompassed my service in the military. That was followed by a career in the railroad industry. Ultimately, the genesis of Sol-Caritas ushered in the period when this man shaped my life.

The curtain had just come down on the production of the most daring comedy shows to hit theaters across the nation. This includes the Will Rogers Coliseum, The Oil Palace, and the renowned Apollo Theater. These were exciting times, full of glamour, notable comics, and celebrities, and of course, the return on my investments was not too bad either. Still, I found myself looking for less risky ways to build my company.

At the time, Jeff was the General Manager of the Houston Improv. His reputation as "challenging to deal with" preceded him. I'd soon find out that was not the case at all. Prior to meeting Mr. Sewell for the first time, I played it safe. My mother was a stickler for first impressions. This was a woman who insisted I wear a three-piece suit to my job interview at McDonald's the day before my sixteenth birthday. I channeled her sense of formality and donned formal attire for my visit with Mr. Sewell at the Improv.

I had shared my aspirations with a few individuals who had deep ties within the industry. They cast doubts, tried to deter me, and all but assured me that my efforts would be futile. Their reasons varied, but for the most part, a few naysayers asserted that the Improv produced its own shows and this exclusivity meant they would have no interest in collaborating with me. This proved to be completely wrong!

Following that meeting, I'd go on to collaborate with the Improv for over 15 years, producing over 300 comedy and poetry shows, and building a friendship with Jeff that is strong to this day; a friendship that transcends the Improv!

That pivotal decision, so many years ago, irrevocably transformed the trajectory of my life.

Both Gil and Jeff provided platforms for me to express my artistry as a performer and a producer. They also played an instrumental role in inspiring me to write my third book. This work of fiction, a departure from my traditional narratives, is another literary labor of love, an odyssey I hope enthralls, intrigues, and informs.

I am forever grateful to Bro. Gil and Mr. Sewell for guiding me to this incredible new phase of what has been a very blessed life.

FOREWORD

As a psychology professor, I am deeply impressed by Carlos Wallace's latest work, "Why Sell Lies When the Truth Is Free." This book transcends traditional narratives by delving into the intricate facets of human dynamics, heredity, love, and personal identity. Wallace's fearless exploration of harsh realities such as racism and mental health challenges provides a valuable platform for reflection and discussion, making it a crucial read for anyone interested in the complexities of the human experience. The gradual reveal of hidden secrets adds an element of suspense and depth to the narrative, keeping readers engaged from start to finish. "Why Sell Lies When the Truth Is Free" is a thought-provoking, emotionally charged masterpiece that exemplifies the resilience of the human spirit when faced with adversity. Carlos Wallace's contribution to literature deserves high praise for its insightful exploration of the human condition and its potential to impact readers in a profound and transformative manner.

Dr. Cherry Sawyerr, Psy.D
Clinical Psychology Professor
Prairie View A&M University

CONTENTS

It's difficult to be honest with others when you continue lying to yourself.

CARLOS WALLACE

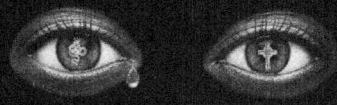

PROLOGUE

"

Imagination judges the future by the past but concerns itself with the future more than with the past.

NAPOLEON HILL

learned valuable lessons from my childhood that shaped my behavior and character. These teachings inspired me to write my first book, "*Life Is Not Complicated - YOU ARE*," which has sold over half a million copies to date. If you told me years ago that I would write my third book before I was 55 years old, I would not have believed it.

An active life has a way of changing your mind and revolutionizing your perspective.

I have experienced so much since writing "*Life Is Not Complicated.*" Events and personal growth have reframed my outlook, sharpened my views on existing beliefs, and compelled me to document my thoughts again.

This time, I changed my writing style a bit! Even I was amazed at the final product.

When I sat down to write "*Why Sell Lies When the Truth Is Free*," I was aware the storyline, characters, and tone of the book would stir controversy. Never one to shy away from topics known to divide nations, ignite arguments at the dinner table, challenge the foundations of our political structure, and disrupt conversations from barber shops to Capitol Hill, I went into the writing process full throttle! This time, I push boundaries, test limits, and stretch my creativity to create a narrative that challenges readers to think beyond the normal scope of societal norms.

While this decision carries an element of risk, I am not deterred. Anything that questions conventional wisdom is bound to be provocative.

I welcome potential backlash. Let's start a conversation!

Now more than ever, we must engage in talks about race, relationships, socioeconomic disparities, mental health, and politics if we ever hope to uncover the root causes of the problems that afflict our families and hinder leadership on a local, national, and federal level.

"*Why Sell Lies When the Truth is Free*" will compel readers to ask tough questions about themselves and others. Each chapter will sow a deeply thought-provoking seed that will resonate in your mind long after you've turned the final page. After all, the pursuit of knowledge and understanding should be timeless and serve as one of the few constants in our lives.

Those who read my first two books know I do not claim to have all the answers, but I believe certain fundamentals endure.

A healthy upbringing is the foundation for good families, productive communities, progressive political cultures, and decent human beings. It all begins at home, and I firmly stand by this belief. Moreover, raising sons who embody honor, dignity, fearlessness, respect, and intelligence is vital. Boys and young men should understand that not every battle is theirs to fight and that it takes courage to walk away from situations they may not win.

Similarly, we must raise daughters who are intelligent, savvy, and strong; girls and young women who value their lives and recognize their critical role in the lives of others.

Shielding children from the harsh realities of the world does them a disservice.

These teachings, however, are not sufficient. It is not enough to know about the "principles." One must also identify when values and ethics are being perverted, twisted, and exploited. I often wonder if most people are ready to deal with the effects of deceit?

That is why the message in "*Why Sell Lies When the Truth is Free*" is so important.

In my opinion, truth, transparency, accountability, trust, and loyalty must also be woven into the fabric of every life if we, as a society, community, or country, will ever evolve past our current state of conflict. Embracing truth is the conduit to freedom, enlightenment, and advancement. Ignoring truth won't silence reality. Truth persists, undeterred. Our most potent response is to confront it, glean wisdom from its revelations, and drive it forward.

History abounds with examples of individuals who never transcended savagery. We often cannot recognize this behavior because we are too preoccupied with evading reality. Regrettably, many of these people are our neighbors, religious and political leaders, and even family members. "*Why Sell Lies When the Truth is Free*" challenges the reader to reflect on this behavior and, hopefully, sheds light on the perils of living lives defined by falsehoods. On a deeply personal level, this book will remind you to always arm yourselves with awareness and become so attuned to what is happening in the world (and your lives) that you have no choice but to ask questions! Embrace the roles of truth-seekers, risk-takers, and champions of accountability. Doing this will help you confront adversity, injustice, suffering, and unpredictability with greater resilience and understanding.

While I may not single-handedly change the world with one book (or three), I can impart the lessons I've learned and the knowledge I've gathered and encourage others to do the same.

Hopefully, "*Why Sell Lies When the Truth is Free*" inspires curiosity, defiance, and outrage in one's constant search for truth.

PARALYZED

CHAPTER 1

"

Let a man avoid
evil deeds as a
man who loves life
avoids poison.

BUDDHA

I was awakened by the bright beam of an unforgiving sun. A piercing light radiated through the shades, falling across my face in what I'm sure were fragmented prisms that irritated my eyes. Squinting, I struggled to adjust my gaze. Judging by the temperature, one thing's for sure: it was going to be a hot, sunny day.

With everything going on in my life, I definitely was not complaining about the promise of a beautiful day. Those have been very rare.

I lay in bed for another 10 minutes, catching up on much-needed rest. I tried to raise my head off the pillow. Something was wrong. I struggled against some unknown pressure. I could not pick my head up.

My eyes widened as I surveyed the room.

"Calm down," I whispered to myself.

I took a deep breath and steadied myself, convinced I probably slept awkwardly and got a crick in my neck. I tried again. My neck felt like it would snap under the pressure of this inexplicable weight.

Did I strain a muscle?

I tried again.

No luck.

Panic struck.

Suddenly, I couldn't feel any part of my body. All I could do was blink. And breathe. Even that was getting shallow!

What was wrong with me?

I lay still, willing my muscles to comply.

My breathing intensified. I struggled to gain mobility. Had I not been breathing so hard, I would have thought I was close to death.

Am I having some kind of out-of-body experience?

I felt something hot singe my skin. Heat was consuming me. What the hell could this...

"Jesus Christ, it's the sun," I exclaimed.

I shifted and peered through the half-open shades. To my horror, I saw the huge, glowing sphere of hat gas moving closer to my window.

This doesn't make sense. Is the sun falling out of the sky? What the hell is going on?

I needed help. I struggled to push air from my lungs, through my larynx, and out of my mouth. Nothing was working.

Suddenly, I heard a voice yelling.

"Move! Get up!"

I paused for a second, although it felt like an hour. Was that sound in my head or coming from my mouth?

Fear caught in my throat. I started choking. Seconds later, I felt like I was suffocating. The pressure in my heart began building.

The **pounding grew frantic.** Every valve must have been pumping desperately. The sun got closer. My skin was melting. I knew, within minutes, it would come crashing through my roof and burn me alive.

"Get up! For the love of God, get up," I pleaded with myself.

I wasn't sure if my cries had become as useless as my incapacitated body. I couldn't look directly into the source of my impending doom.

I decided I would not give up. I may perish in this surreal, apocalyptic, end of days scenario, but not without a fight. **I plan to die like I lived: Fearlessly!**

I shouted at the top of my lungs, **"Dammit, get up, get up…save yourself! Get up! On your feet! On your feet! On your feet!"**

Finally, my brain reacted. Rapid-fire synapses ignited. **My body responded.** Slowly, the feeling in my arms, legs, fingers, and toes began coming back. A tingle, a twitch, a reflex.

I shot out of bed like a bullet from the barrel of a gun. I was hot, sweating, and still yelling, "**On your feet…!**"

Wait, was I?

Hold on. Who the hell is yelling?

The voice echoed through the atmosphere (through me) like a clap of thunder…

"**On…**"

"**Your…**"

"**Feet…!**"

Reality set in.

"Shit, I'm having a nightmare!"

I looked around frantically. The clock on the wall read exactly 4.30 a.m.

I heard it again. There was no mistaking from where that booming order emanated.

"**On your feet!**"

The Company Commander's rally cry was loud and clear.

There is (and will never be) nothing more jarring at this ungodly hour of the morning than the soul-snatching sound of an officer intent on getting your attention. You'd think this man- all five feet, eight inches of him- was using a megaphone. The sound of this guy's voice could easily wake the dead. Given the nightmare I had before being roused so abruptly from my sleep, he practically did.

"It is 4.30 a.m., people!" he yelled. **"Wake up! Now! Don't make me say that shit again!"**

I heard grunts, sighs, and moans. Eighty other men, also not accustomed to such a full-throated wake-up call, started making a mad dash to do whatever needed to comply. We had not been fully indoctrinated yet but understood that we better do as we were told. My shipmates and I rushed to get up and at attention, and my new life had begun. I was now in the United States Navy, and we hit the deck early every day.

I was nervous (and slightly uncertain) about my decision. However, I was ready for whatever challenges lay ahead. I chose this. No one forced me. I didn't enlist on a dare. I did my research and talked extensively to recruiters, questioning them about every scenario.

"How long is boot camp?"

"Where will I be stationed?"

"What if I get hurt?"

"Can I earn college credit?"

That last inquiry was to appease my mother. **She was adamant about me going to college.** She was not keen on a career path that involved guns, ships, combat, and war. My decision baffled her. Of all the things I could do with my life, **I joined the Navy.**

When I mustered up the courage to tell her I enlisted, the look on her face fluctuated between confusion, disbelief, and rage.

Ultimately, rage prevailed.

After berating me with a barrage of expletives and questions like, **"How could you throw your life away like this?"** and, **"Didn't we agree you would become an engineer?"**

I never had an opportunity to answer.

"Who the hell put you up to this foolishness?" "Did you forget that in this house, we go to college!" and **"If you go through with this, you understand that I will never speak to you again?"**

She stormed out of the kitchen.

I sat there, slack-jawed. I never considered my decision would cause so much pain. My grandfather had been an admiral. He was a decorated officer who led his fleet during World War II. My father followed in his footsteps, serving in Vietnam. Why was she so shocked? I could only assume she wanted me to break the cycle. Deep down, I felt my mother blamed the Navy for turning my father into the bastard he was. Lord forbid her son to suffer the same fate.

Nonetheless, I had to do it because (ironically) I wanted to put as much distance between my father and me as the military put between him and Mom. Those two were on opposite ends of the spectrum. He was a jerk. She was the kindest soul you'd ever meet. At this point, nothing could bridge the gap between them.

They say war does something to a man. It changes him. The battles waged on the front line turn inward. Friends and family become strangers caught in the crossfire. Honestly, I think my father was born an angry, raging lunatic. I used to admire him before he showed us his true colors.

I signed up without my momma's blessing. To this day, that was one of the hardest decisions I ever made.

The first day was pretty much what I expected. I didn't set my bar too high to account for disruptions. Expectations don't always measure up. Like other experiences in my life, I understood that just because I imagined what was about to happen, that didn't mean it would play out that way.

"Port side, you have twenty minutes to brush your teeth, wash your face, and shave before reporting to your bunks. Starboard side, you have twenty minutes to make your bunks, and there will be an inspection. Count on it."

All this hustle and bustle and the relentless squawking made me wonder whether my mother was right. Would a quieter, more predictable life be so bad? I should have taken a bunch of college courses, earned a degree, and lived a safe, stable existence. I might be content following someone else's dreams.

The thought was fleeting. I knew I'd made the right decision. I wanted to prove that all the men in my family were not weapons-grade assholes.

I must have drifted into my own world because the next sound I heard snapped me out of my stupor so unexpectedly I almost choked on the toothpaste.

"Ruane, stop daydreaming and get your bunk squared away immediately!"

"This isn't Kentucky, son! Get it together before I drop you!"

Well, he was definitely right about one thing: this place, San Diego, was nothing like my hometown!

I was a good ol' boy from Paducah, Kentucky, a city with a population of about twenty-five thousand. Our biggest claim to fame? We won the Great American Main Street Award and became an Accredited Kentucky Main Street Community. I realize this is probably small potatoes to folks in Silicon Beach, but it is a major source of pride to us.

We often joked that the early French and American settlers who erected the town's first framed buildings and William Clark (who named our fair city) would be relieved we received an award. They probably believed we'd be cursed for misspelling the name of the Padouca Indian Tribe. Padouca was one of four tribes inhabiting the region in the early 1800s. The historic contribution of Native Americans is still apparent throughout our city.

Thankfully, Clark's faux pas wasn't used against our beloved hometown. At least not in obvious ways.

Growing up in a city where two rivers and a 340-foot transient boat dock remain a prominent source of industry, I'd been around water and ships all my life. I was destined to become a third-generation sailor, and I would wear the designation with pride.

The next eight weeks would define the rest of my adult life in ways I'd never imagined.

The road that led me to this military base, a world away from the town where I grew up, was full of disappointment, shattered dreams, and unexpected twists and turns. I prayed I chose the right path.

"I want to see everyone in formation at exactly zero-five-ten. If anyone is late, there will be consequences for everyone."

My name is Martin Ruane III. My life, shall we say, has been complicated.

FINDING SOLACE IN THE NAVY

CHAPTER 2

"

Silence is safer than speech.

EPICTETUS

B eing underway was the greatest experience of my life. Standing on that mammoth vessel reminded me how far I'd traveled from my "regular" life.

The ship cut through the choppy sea smooth as a hot knife through butter, like sharpened blades gliding across glass. Despite the size of the vast structure, there is a stoic elegance about it. If I listened closely, I could hear the hull displace the water, allowing the ship to dominate the ocean to reign supreme over the earth's surface. The water exacts enough force to erode the land, yet it submits to the authority of our ship. Every time I stand on the outer deck of this massive vessel, looking out at the sea, I am lost in these reflections.

Amazing. I was in awe.

Every once in a while, though, I reminded myself that, while it was extraordinary, growing up in a rural community and living a simple life was not all bad. What my upbringing lacked in excitement, it more than made up for in establishing a sense of belonging. I found comfort in knowing local shop owners, seeing former teachers at Walmart, and hearing the latest gossip while pumping gas. Back then, it never even occurred to me I was missing out on anything. You know what you know and, more importantly, can't miss what you never had.

I knew I wanted something more and believed that I needed to expand my horizons.

Each day, I breathed in the salt air and marveled at the endless expanse of the ocean stretching beyond the vista. I knew I would experience natural wonders like sunrises in the Mediterranean and sunsets in the South Pacific. This is what I yearned for. The peace, the adventure, the discovery.

Not bad for a Kentuckian from small-town America.

Life on an amphibious assault ship was surreal. I simplified the description for my mom sometimes, explaining that our aviation facilities host helicopters to support forces ashore. "It's like being in a floating city powered by state-of-the-art technology and equipment, Mom. Every day is a new adventure. We're constantly training and preparing for any mission that may come our way."

The adrenaline rush of being aboard the USS Dubuque LPD-8 was addictive. I hit the ground running, too, training in my rate immediately after basic training. I operated and maintained the Navy's global satellite telecommunications and micro-computer systems, mainframe computers, and the fleet's local and wide area networks. Whenever a civilian asked what I did, that is exactly what I told them. No shame. At all. Nothing boosts your ego like being part of the unit that keeps critical, high-level, top-secret information for the U.S. Navy on point.

I shared all this with my mom each time we talked, and no matter how crazy, fascinating, or moving the story was, the conversation ended the same way:

"Please be safe, Marty, don't be a hero!" she'd say.

"Nah, we leave that to the Marines!"

That got a laugh out of her every time.

She would write to me religiously, and I sent her souvenirs from my travels. I imagined her showing off to all her friends, displaying all the gifts I've sent her. I was grateful to provide distractions, something to look forward to. She was always busy caring for my brother Lance, who is severely autistic, or tending to my jerk of a father, so bringing some sense of joy to her life feels good.

Watching my mother with Lance was always bittersweet. It's as if love and nurturing co-mingled with crushing challenges. **Every day, I marveled at my mom's unwavering devotion.** I don't know how she did it. Even though he tested her patience, she poured her heart and soul into caring for Lance. **The older I got, the more I could tell that the weight of her responsibilities was taking an emotional toll on her.**

A few years ago, I learned my mom harbored the belief my father somehow blamed her for the fact my brother was imperfect in his eyes. Imagine that. A man laden with obvious insecurities and frustrations, channeling his anger toward her in vile words and actions.

I did the best I could to help her with Lance. Deep down, I regret not doing more.

I made zero attempts to keep in touch with my father. Our back-and-forth before I left for boot camp made that pretty easy.

He didn't even try to understand my desire to move away from home.

"The *what?*"

"The Navy, Dad. I leave tomorrow."

"Finally, a smart decision. Glad I lived long enough to see you make one of those."

"Real supportive, Dad."

"Yeah, well, whatever. Just don't fuck this up."

I changed the focus of the conversation to avoid another fight.

"Mom isn't too happy about it."

"She probably feels like you're abandoning your family. You've always been selfish. Selfish and hard-headed, so what did you expect?"

What a joke. My father pretending to care that I hurt my mother.

"Seriously, Dad, you think college is stupid. Now, you can't even find something decent to say about me joining the military. If I gave a damn what you thought, I'd be pretty confused!"

"You make a lot of dumb choices, Marty, and it comes back to bite you in the ass, and we have to clean up your mess. At least I can get behind this."

The nerve of this guy. We are all screwed up because of him and his decisions!

Years ago, I learned to accept that he lived in a world where he felt he could do or say hurtful things to us. Still, when you turn the tables on him and shine a mirror in his face, he reverts to his manipulative mind game. All our lives, he twisted our words and perverted our emotions to make us sound crazy. His behavior was unnerving, and some days bordered on sociopathic.

Thank God I got away from this narcissistic prick.

I think back to the day I arrived in Japan. Let's just say anyone watching me and seeing my reaction could tell I hadn't been to many places. The sights, sounds, and smells nearly floored me when I stepped off the plane. Everywhere I turned, there was some amazing discovery overwhelming my senses. I didn't blink for the first hour!

I felt so small standing among Tokyo's towering skyscrapers and neon lights. I even saw ancient temples and the gardens of Kyoto. It was like being transported to a different world at every turn.

I was four years in, but the feeling never got old. Every adventure was one more memory away from home. The more I lived, the faster recollections of my bitter, troubled past died. I shed pain like snakes shed their skin. Ironically, this chapter of my life mimicked the reptile's transformation.

I remember reading that, as snakes grow, their skin no longer accommodates their altered state. Their eyes start to look opaque or clouded because the newly formed covering obscures them. Since they have trouble seeing during this time, they hide until a new outer layer emerges, free of parasites and other organisms that could harm the host.

Their eyesight also returns. The funny thing is, for years, I tried to turn a blind eye to painful memories.

My eyesight always returned.

One night, when I was alone with my thoughts, listening to the sound of the water, I began to reflect. I thought back to the days when my mother was happy. Her laugh was infectious. She could sow hope in the worst circumstances. Because she was typically so ebullient, the shift in her demeanor was obtrusive.

I can pinpoint to the second the moment her soul died.

The argument was violent. The words exchanged between my mom and dad were too traumatic for a ten-year-old, yet there I was, in the line of fire. An unwitting victim.

The shouts from downstairs were muffled, so I could barely hear what was said. I got out of bed slowly so no one knew I was listening. I put my ear to the door and caught a word or two here and there.

"Liar!" my mother screamed, her voice cracking.

"Calm down, you're going to wake the boys!"

The conversation continued, choppy, laced with anger.

"You are self-righteous, hypocritical..."

I couldn't understand the last few words.

My father's response was loud and clear.

"You're lucky I didn't just leave your ass..."

His language was as hurtful as a dull knife cutting through a vein.

I heard my father trying to justify his actions. I could not comprehend what he had done to reduce my mother to tears. At one point, he blamed her for "making him" betray his family. Her sobs came in rapid bursts, and I was sure she stopped breathing for seconds at a time. I could sense she was losing control. I wanted to come to her rescue, but he sounded so angry I feared what he'd do to me.

My father's hostility spread like wildfire from that point on. He acted like he had license to dole out vitriol with impunity and took it out on my mother and me. The older (and bigger I got), the less I tolerated it. Every year, my hatred for him grew until I was so consumed by loathing I couldn't stand to be in the same state or breathe the same air he did. There is no greater shame than being related to a man void of decency and basic humanity.

If I never see him again, it will be too soon.

The tougher this Kentuckian skin becomes, the more evolved my thinking gets. Meeting folks from diverse backgrounds has been the greatest life lesson. I've seen the best and the worst of new cultures. War-torn countries where everyone is struggling to survive, and the devastation is profound. I've witnessed the destruction of conflict firsthand and the toll it takes on the population and the land. It's a sobering reminder of why we do what we do.

None of that keeps painful memories at bay, though. I was hundreds of miles away at sea but not completely detached. I know my mom was still in a miserable marriage, my brother will always be mentally challenged, and my father...well, will not stop being an asshole.

There is no escaping any of that.

I was leaving chow one night when I got the order to see the Chaplain. He had received a message from the American Red Cross Emergency Communications Service. My heart sank. I immediately thought something had happened to my brother.

The Chaplain's voice was even but sympathetic.

"We regret to inform you..."

AN UNSPOKEN EULOGY

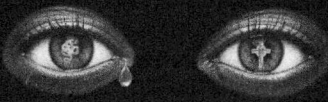

CHAPTER 3

"

Life doesn't make any sense without interdependence. We need each other, and the sooner we learn that the better for us all.

ERIK ERIKSON

The brisk air assaulted my dry skin. I could feel the frigid temperatures settle into my bones. This was the coldest day on record for Paducah. The parts of my body that had become accustomed to warmer climates felt numb. But that did not keep my teeth from chattering or hide the chills that ran up my spine and through my extremities. I actually missed soaking in sweat, the heat coating me from head to toe.

Considering how cold-hearted my father was, I guess the arctic climate was fitting.

I will never get used to this. So much had changed.

For four years, my military service kindled a cultural awareness I was not expecting. My view of the world and its diverse, ever-evolving human race was altered. Given the principles I had grown up believing in the so-called real world my father convinced me I lived in, I was stunned to discover how my state of mind had changed. I was literally working through a withdrawal, detoxing from the misinformation and hate that had overwhelmed my senses for years. This deprogramming progressed as I sailed over five thousand miles from my base in Yokosuka, Japan, and spent time in Asia and India. This geographical expedition on the military's dime taught me so much.

I finally arrived at the church. Memories of Sunday services flooded my mind. The pastor's bombastic sermons.

My mother sitting there nervously, her mind clearly elsewhere. Her legs crossed at the ankles, hands wringing in her lap. I would see her lips moving, but it was never in time with anything happening on the pulpit or the choir loft. It was just her own private prayers. Silent cries for what? Mercy? Forgiveness? Redemption? My father sat beside her, clueless. Or maybe not. He was never the most compassionate man. It would not surprise me if he knew my mother had withdrawn into herself and was happy. She was somewhere, anywhere; she could not bother him. I often wish she had taken me to that place inside her mind where she escaped each week.

The warmth of the church provided welcome relief from the cold. The pews were packed with people, some of whom (to my confusion) admired him. Of course, some wanted to rip his heart out and crush it with their bare hands. Many were there because he was dead, while quite a few were there to make sure that was indeed the case.

When I was young, my father told me something I hadn't understood until today. He said, **"When I die, those who care enough to attend my funeral will be divided. Half will be there to weep and mourn. The others will check my pulse in the casket to make sure I'm gone."**

Count me among the latter.

As I surveyed the people in the church and tried to discern who was there (and why), I thought it was just like my father to throw daggers from his final resting place. Even in death, he got in your head. I spotted my mother lovingly assisting my brother (without Ms. Elnora) as they took the solemn walk through the aisles, eyes fixed on the coffin. This was undoubtedly an effort to avoid those stares of pity and, possibly, condemnation. We were all going to be seated in the front row. I dreaded the juxtaposition of mourners and the unloved departed. I felt like we were sideshow freaks, part of a morbid circus where people gawked at us and passed judgment. The designated pew was supposed to make us feel special. I felt like a caged animal. I never shed a tear despite everyone's expectations. My father had died. Surely, I should be grieving. But I resisted the urge to perform. I sat there with my family under the mourners' watchful eyes. Some waiting for me to cry, others willing me to do so.

I hadn't seen some of these folks since my high school graduation. I thought I'd never see them again after I crossed that stage and received my diploma. I left shortly after the ceremony, not intending to return to this miserable town. The more I sailed to beautiful countries and indulged in rich cultures, the faster memories of home faded.

Mom was the only person I missed, although we talked frequently over the last four years. I couldn't let her down. I'm a mama's boy and proud of it! Every week, at least one letter would make its way to me. I called frequently to share my latest exciting adventures. Lately, while the letters were still consistent, they seemed shorter. My mom explained she had become overwhelmed; my brother required so much more attention and so much of her time.

For reasons unbeknownst to me, Ms. Elnora was no longer working for her. **She had been a part of our family for years, and then, just like that, she was gone.** I found her absence odd, but I did not ask questions.

We walked by each pew, slowly and deliberately, as if trudging through quicksand toward our ultimate punishment, a death sentence. At least, that is how it seemed. Whispers sounded like screams. The stone-faced stares belied questions, concerns, doubts, and pity.

I couldn't bring myself to look at my mom. **What would happen to her now? My father was her lifeline** (the irony of that statement does not escape me). She never worked outside our home. **Caring for Lance, a low-functioning autistic, was a full-time job.** My father was a prideful man, a poster child for narcissism. **He would not allow my mom to be anything but a homemaker or a mother.** He was controlling, plain and simple.

That is one of the many things he and I clashed over. He was a stubborn brute, completely unwilling to evolve past primal proclivities. He was set in his ways, trapped in a time warp. His death should have freed us. Instead, the memory of his abuse, his hatred, and his racism held us captive.

Finally, we arrived at our designated seats. The front row. I glanced at Mom and made sure she was okay before I zoned out. She was so focused on making my brother comfortable, she barely had time to shed a tear. The pastor stepped up to the pulpit, and I knew the agonizing eulogy was about to begin. He looked at ease. How many of these had he done? He wasted no time. The reading was from Psalm 145.

> *"Great is the Lord and greatly to be praised, and his greatness is unsearchable. My mouth will speak the praise of the Lord and let all flesh bless His holy name forever and ever."*

Oh, brother.

"On behalf of the Ruane family, I welcome those gathered here today." His voice was booming. "We gather to celebrate the life of Martin 'Marty' Ruane, Jr., a well-known and respected pillar of our community."

He sounded rehearsed. This must be the standard opener for every funeral, because he clearly could not be talking about my father.

"A man never at a loss for words and often misunderstood."

Misunderstood? How?

The pastor droned on and on.

I reflected.

My father and I rarely saw eye to eye. As I matured, we remained on opposite sides of every debate. He was old school with traditional values, and I was very progressive. We could not have been more different. It made him so angry, and I reveled in his displeasure.

I crossed him solely to infuriate him. He deserved every ounce of the acrimony I poured into our relationship.

My father's flawed thinking seeped into every aspect of our lives and decision-making. His views confused me and interfered with my daily activities.

Every Friday night, I did battle on the gridiron with teammates he referred to as **"brothers from the other side of the tracks."** We took the field and faced off against our opponents, sharing dreams of playing on Sundays, millions of fans shouting our names and wearing our jerseys. Race wasn't an issue. Our team slogan was "One Team–One Mission." Our coaches drilled that into our psyche. That's probably why I adapted to modern Navy life so seamlessly. The values of inclusion, acceptance, and teamwork had already been instilled. I resisted my father's propensity toward racism and became immune to his hatred. Despite his divisive nature, I remained the same, even keeled, accepting man I willed myself to be.

Ironically, my father suffered a massive heart attack during, of all things, an NFL game. Once an avid fan, he had become completely disgusted with everything concerning the National Football League. The source of his discontent? "Those goddamned ungrateful, selfish son-of-a-bitch players kneeling during the national anthem."

The controversy drove him mad. NFL players began kneeling during the national anthem following the example set by then-49ers quarterback Colin Kaepernick. They said they were protesting racial inequalities and police violence against minorities in America. Some players stood but raised their fists to show solidarity with Kaepernick. The entire display ran him hot! The proud Vietnam veteran of our family took great offense at this "blatant disrespect for everything he fought for." He would throw things at the television and shout profanities.

It did not help that he was not the only one raging against the players' actions. Millions of fans joined in his outrage. Hell, even President Donald Trump attacked the NFL players who kneeled during the anthem. He spewed outright venom in tweets and statements in late September 2017. His comments resonated with

Americans like my father but also touched a nerve with players and many NFL owners. There was more head-butting off the field than on.

He memorized and often recited the **National Flag Code** adopted on June 14, 1923. He would yell it out during a game... as if the players could hear him.

"The flag should never be carried flat or horizontally, but always aloft and free."

It was an obsession.

"The flag should never be used for advertising purposes in any manner whatsoever."

He took a sip of his beer.

"It should not be embroidered on such articles as cushions or handkerchiefs and the like, printed or otherwise impressed on paper napkins or boxes or anything designed for temporary use and discard."

He threw the remote at the television, barely missing the screen. He'd already destroyed one set. It was a matter of time before he cracked another.

"Advertising signs should not be fastened to a staff or halyard from which the flag is flown."

My mother would leave the room, shaking her head and wringing her hands.

"No part of the flag should ever be used as a costume or athletic uniform. However, a flag patch may be affixed to the uniform of military personnel, firefighters, police officers, and members of patriotic organizations."

He'd shout, to no one in particular, **"You hear that? Are you listening?"**

"The flag represents a living country and is itself considered a living thing. Therefore, the lapel flag pin, being a replica, should be worn on the left lapel near the heart."

By this time, he was standing, beer in his left hand, right hand over his heart, close to tears.

My father never admitted the fact kneeling was not an offense. I had desperately wanted to read the official code myself to find violations that I could use in my own points of view. **To hear that my father took ill during a game...?**

I didn't believe in karma, but if such a thing exists, that was the best example. The kneeling literally stopped his heart.

My mom recounted the events of that day.

She was cooking dinner when she heard a lamp smash on the floor. She sauntered into the living room with no particular sense of urgency, only to find my father slumped over the side of the recliner. I hated that chair. It was his favorite, and there would be hell to pay if anyone ever sat in the thing. Yet, the NFL players were "selfish." The hypocrisy was mind-blowing.

My mother said she shrieked and called his name. No response. Her heart began pounding, and panic set in. She scrambled to call 911 and could barely yell, "Oh my God, help!"

The 911 operator struggled to understand her through her tears and panting cries.

"Get here now! He's not breathing!" she stammered.

As I emerged from my trance, the pastor's words became pointed. "We ask that you continue to pray for the family in this troubled and challenging time." I could feel his eyes peer into my soul.

The pastor sat down. It was time for mourners to share their testimonies. Mom wanted to keep all remarks under two minutes. I suggested no one be allowed to speak at all. I lost that argument.

Fortunately, only four people came forward. I could handle eight minutes. I didn't bother listening to the mindless prattle of people who never knew him and his family.

My thoughts drifted again to the past and lingered on the tough times that defined our relationship. My childhood had been marred by my father's indiscretions. I was actually grateful for at least one thing: my father transformed me into an alpha male, a leader, and a caretaker. He taught me to be responsible, accountable for my actions, and devoted to my views. Even though we disagreed about everything (because he also taught me to be fiercely independent in my thinking), he wanted me to stand firm in my beliefs.

Before the gaping chasm that defined our relationship, he imparted words of wisdom that stuck with me.

"Son, your word is the only thing you can give and keep at the same time," he would say.

Come to think of it, the only decent phrases he knew were clichés. Nevertheless, I wanted to share his valuable knowledge with my child someday. I learned lessons at home I could never have discovered in a classroom.

What a waste.

My mom hissed at me, "Marty, do you want to speak on behalf of the family?" As the "official" man of the house, it was my duty.

I looked right into her eyes for the first time that day and declined. I was worried about what would come flying out of my mouth.

My mind raced. I was overcome with mixed emotions. I reasoned that my conflicted feelings would only confuse people. My younger self might sing his praises as the man who coached my football team. **The older Martin, a former student council president, a high-school football star, a military man, a man who watched his mother suffer and knew more about the world and compassion, would be bitter and rebellious.**

"Are you sure you don't want to go up?" **Mom asked.**

I was sure.

She gave the pastor a slight nod. With that, we began mentally preparing for my dad's journey to his final destination.

My father took immense pride in being a veteran. Many of his friends died after years of failing health.

Their illness was often compounded by the substandard care veterans of the most gruesome wars in our nation's history received. My father had no long-term medical conditions, even after two tours. He used to lament that the Vietnam War produced a generation of homeless vets who flew below the radar. It's as if they were invisible.

I think he suffered a form of survivor's guilt, a veteran who did well while so many of his comrades suffered. My mother said that is why she was so upset when I enlisted. She did not want me to suffer a similar fate, fall victim to sexually transmitted diseases, or succumb to mental health issues like PTSD.

My father's mind and body remained solid until he went into cardiac arrest. One of his closest friends was not so lucky. We attended that man's funeral. I was so young, but I could still see the pain on my father's face. After the funeral, I remembered the Honor Guard presenting his son with a flag. I dreamed of being that boy one day. Don't get me wrong, I didn't want my dad to die. I just appreciated the ceremony, the pomp and circumstance. I thought that was such an honorable way to become a man.

Here I was, a twenty-two-year-old veteran, and I didn't care what they did with that flag.

The Honor Guard approached, and I stood proudly in my navy dress blues. As they lowered the casket, my mom wept, and my brother stared, unaware of what was going on.

Inside my heart, the emotions raged.

I wondered what tomorrow would bring.

DREAM SEQUENCE

"

I know I have plenty of enemies, but I'd rather be the most-hated winning coach in the country than the most-popular losing one.

ADOLPH RUPP

couldn't sleep. No matter how hard I tried, the night just would not end!

I stared out the window and felt like the twinkling lights surrounding the vast ribbon of stars were mocking me. This paranoia has become such a sickening part of my thought process, no matter how much I try to remain positive.

I was finally on the brink of a new chapter—college. Nervousness and excitement coursed through my veins, mingling with an inexplicable ache that tugged at my heart.

As I lay there, pleading with God to cover me with at least a few hours of slumber, something caught my eye. It happened so quickly that I wondered if I had really seen it. I sat up slowly, leaned over the side of the bed, and reached for my .45.

"If somebody is in here, I'm letting you know I'm not aiming to scare you. I will shoot your ass," I warned.

Silence.

I got out of bed and walked to the corner of the room. My mind must be playing tricks on me.

No sooner did I turn to walk back to the bed than I felt a presence wash over the room. The hairs on the back of my neck and my arms stood up!

"What the hell...?"

I turned swiftly, ready to light up whoever was stupid enough to come into my house.

My eyes had already adjusted to the dark, but this could not be who I thought it was.

"Dad?"

The hazy form started to take shape, morphing into the hulking figure I now recognized as the man I hated.

But how? We saw them put him in the ground!

I stared in disbelief, the rage building inside. I was standing face to face with my deceased father, a specter of malevolence.

My eyes blinked rapidly. Rationally, everything inside me said this could not be happening, but it felt real. I was so unsure that I kept my gun trained on the figure, just in case.

He stood there, wearing the solid black suit my mother had picked out for him. He still resembled the withered corpse we buried, his face sunken, pale, and discolored.

I reached out to touch him, hoping to confirm I was dreaming.

I had to be, right?

I came within an inch of the menacing figure, and, as if on cue, he discharged a barrage of venomous words that ripped through my consciousness with a force deadlier than the bullets in the gun I was too afraid to discharge.

Even in death, his toxic presence loomed.

***"This ain't nothing but the devil,"** I said aloud.*

My father picked up where he left off, berating me, proclaiming I would never amount to anything. He mocked my mother's pain and reveled in the emotional and mental destruction he wreaked on our family.

My anger surged. I lunged at the ghostly figure, desperate to strike out and silence the laughter. In my frenzied state, I stumbled.

I never hit the floor or any foundation that could stop my fall; just continued to plummet through the air while he battered me with taunts.

He laughed mockingly at my futile attempts to retaliate. Every blow I attempted missed its mark. I couldn't touch him. I couldn't hurt him like he had hurt us. He was winning. He was always winning. Hate has no moral compass, and the man who hates as coldly as my father would never feel the sting of regret or lost love.

Even in death...

Moments before my freefall ended in tragedy, I woke with a jolt, soaked in sweat. My body trembled with fear and frustration. The hold my father had on me was undeniable. Scars ran deep. I realized past demons would not be easily vanquished.

PSYCHOLOGY 2301

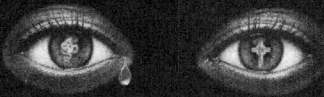

CHAPTER 4

"

Remember, remember always, that all of us, and you and I especially, are descended from immigrants and revolutionists.

FRANKLIN D. ROOSEVELT

C ollege was my chance to break free, forge my own path, and create a better future.

As I stepped onto campus, I clung to hope. I was intent on finding the strength to confront any of my demons and keep defining my destiny. I refused to let my past dictate the future.

The sun shined on the first day of school. There were a lot of smiles and, of course, the typical stressed-out incoming students already fearing the worst rushing past, a pile of books hanging precariously in their arms.

I felt a pang of regret when I ran across a throng of students greeting high school pals. I'd been out of the loop for so long. It didn't help that I was starting college years after my high school comrades. The ones who made it through college graduated and were on to the next phase of their lives.

Those feelings aside, I was finally walking the campus grounds of my dreams. Not many people know this, but I longed to attend this school. I would reenact this day so many times, right down to how I would dress, what I planned on studying, and where I would live! As the years progressed and life got…complicated…those aspirations drifted into the background.

The University of Kentucky. I was taking it all in.

The school has a rich history. I spent years filling my brain with every detail I could retain. I never thought anyone would understand my obsession, so I stored these facts away, but they were always on the tip of my tongue.

I connected with the school on many levels, maybe because I always felt its existence mirrored my life. At least, that is how I reconciled it in my head!

I'd reason that the school and I evolved from humble beginnings.

Long before the University of Kentucky became the symbol of NCAA basketball, representing the basketball-crazed "Bluegrass State," the state of Kentucky birthed the institution under a different name: The Agricultural and Mechanical College of Kentucky University. That was way back in 1865. I'd joke it was like discovering Kobe Bryant (my favorite athlete) had a corny alter ego before becoming the greatest player to ever play the game of basketball.

I wondered how many of my fellow students (especially those four years my junior and leaving home for the first time) knew or cared about all this.

Still, attending this school made my mother extremely happy. However, that was not enough to assuage my reservations. I was filled with endless questions. Would I fit in with a younger crowd with a worldview they inherited from their parents? How many of them have seen what I've seen?

I pushed my doubts down. Most of these students came to school ready to take on the curriculum and conquer the next four years. If they could succeed in this environment, I could, too.

First class, Psychology 2301.

I entered the lecture hall and was met with rows of students. I could tell many of them were already forming cliques. I wasn't surprised to see the ones in the front rows had their noses buried in their textbooks (most likely, they downloaded the curriculum weeks before class began). Others talked and laughed with each other.

Slowly, I walked up the lecture hall steps, trying to find a seat in the crowded room. I couldn't decide whether to be in the back of the class or venture into the middle aisle and settle in among loud, chatty students.

Note to self: stop making everything so hard. I sat toward the back and took in the bird's eye view of the classroom.

Good choice.

The double doors at the front of the classroom creaked open. The talking stopped as everyone watched our professor enter the room. She was not quite what I expected.

Her name was Dr. Cherry Sawyerr, which I learned the night before when I received her syllabus via email. She had a heavy coat over her left arm and a briefcase in her right hand. She greeted us with a quick good morning and a pleasant smile and began setting up her desk. I must admit, she personified professionalism in her tailored pantsuit and hair tied back into a tight bun.

I took my books out of my bag and placed them on the table in front of me.

"Welcome, class; I am Dr. Sawyerr."

"Good morning," we replied, a hodgepodge of voices, tones, and moods.

She sighed after she finished organizing her workspace. A mix of relief and exasperation.

I feel you, Dr. Sawyerr, I thought to myself.

"The first thing you should know is, I want you all to have an open mind."

I've been around long enough to know if someone is asking you to have an open mind, they are about to throw something unorthodox at you.

I braced myself.

"Try to recognize your views of others and, perhaps, abandon some of your learned behavior. In doing so, you may just unlock something about yourself that you didn't realize was there."

She had my attention. I didn't know if it was what she said or how she said it, but her energy kept me riveted.

"The potential of greatness is in you, and it's my job to assist you in discovering it," she said.

She lost me there. It's Psychology. What kind of potential could I glean from that? Id, ego, superego. Done. Next.

I was already off track.

As she continued her introduction, I sat with my chin in my hand. She went on forever. My initial level of attention had waned. Just as I was about to zone her out, she clapped her hands.

I hope that wasn't meant just for me.

"Okay, everyone," she said, "I'm going to set you up in pairs for the first assignment."

The groans flooded the air.

"Okay, okay…I get it," she said with a smirk. "But believe me, there is a method to this exercise."

More like a method to this madness, I thought.

"I'm breaking you out of your comfort zone. Cut those proverbial umbilical cords, people! This is your opportunity to get to know each other. If you're going to succeed in this class, you must push yourself beyond your normal limits."

The now overly enthusiastic professor began calling out names in pairs. I waited patiently to hear mine. I can't say for sure, but it seemed like she intentionally paired us with people whose interests did not quite parallel ours! How she made the connections after being in our presence for less than ten minutes was beyond me, but I figured she'd been doing this long enough to know.

She matched me with an inner-city African-American woman from Chicago.

As soon as Dr. Sawyerr announced our names, we spotted each other. She had been a couple of rows down and immediately made a beeline toward me. I barely had time to move my books and make room for her to sit next to me before she was in my space.

She literally occupied every bit of my personal space.

This was going to be interesting.

She wasted no time sizing me up. She gave me a *thorough* once over, using only her eyes. It was unnerving. I felt like she was doing some kind of deep character diagnostic. I resisted the urge to become defensive as I had so often done when my father looked at me critically.

After a few seconds, she let out a casual **"Hmph."**

I could picture her thinking, **"Oh well, it is what it is."**

When she spoke, her voice was deep, and her tone confident. I could tell she was a force to be reckoned with.

"**I guess we're stuck with each other,**" the girl said, plopping into the seat beside me. "How's it going?"

I extended my hand, waiting for the obligatory handshake. She looked at me like I was an alien.

This academic coupling is off to a rocky start.

I withdrew the courteous formality and used my unshaken hand to open my notebook. I subtly tried to study her thick, dark hair. Her hair was styled in an intricate design of micro braids that looked like it took days to complete. She wore stylish distressed jeans and a fitted sweater that appeared hand-knitted.

"I don't think I caught your name," I said, hoping I did not offend her.

"Alicen," she snapped.

That took me by surprise.

"**Look, can we just get this assignment over with?**" she continued. "**There is truly no need for small talk. I just want an A. Then we can move on.**"

Dr. Sawyerr succeeded in matching the two least compatible people in the world.

The silent treatment Alicen proposed did not last long. As soon as we got acclimated to the arrangement, she started telling me her life story.

I… was not…ready.

In between shuffling papers, discussing the work, and sizing each other up, Alicen shared that she lost her brother to gang violence. I'm not sure why this bothered me so much because I had heard this kind of thing before. Maybe the familiar refrain elicited this uneasy feeling in my gut.

When will this cycle of violence in urban communities end, Jesus?

I was happy to hear she was the first in her family who didn't choose crime as a pastime. Instead, she decided to go to college and change the trajectory of her legacy.

We at least had that in common.

Another similarity we shared was that our mothers were both stay-at-home moms.

The parental connection ended there.

Alicen's father was a proud union machinist. He raised her to be strong and independent (I picked up on that as soon as we met). They were close, but she admits the relationship was challenging at times.

By the end of the class, I had learned that her favorite color was blue, and she liked country and hip-hop music. She wanted to study the mind because she was passionate about understanding others. She talked so much that I forgot the assignment!

Oddly enough, I hung on to her every word. She spoke with authority but was still soft and feminine. She was graceful, yet different from girls who only cared about fashion, makeup, and fresh nail sets.

Before we knew it, class was over, and everyone was scrambling to make it to the next lecture on time.

"You want to meet at the library tomorrow to work on our assignment," she asked as she gathered her supplies.

"Sure," I replied awkwardly. "Tell me what time, and I'll be there."

I am unsure when I was this yielding with anyone, much less a woman I had just met.

We set a time, said goodbye, and went our separate ways.

When I got back to my dorm, I reviewed the assignment requirements. We had to read a book called *"Life Is Not Complicated – YOU ARE."* Professor Sawyerr described it as a common ice-breaker novel by author Carlos Wallace. She raved about it, calling it a life changer. I'll be the judge of that.

We also had to outline Abraham Maslow's hierarchy of needs in his "A Theory of Human Motivation." The focus here was on theories of developmental psychology and homed in on a classification system that considers the universal needs of society as its base and then delves into the complexities of more acquired emotions.

It's going to be a long ass semester.

The day Alicen and I were supposed to meet, I got to the library at 3:55 p.m. You can take the man out of the military, but you can't... well, you know.

While I waited for her to arrive, I could still hear her voice ringing in my ears. I could not quite pinpoint exactly what I was feeling. Part of me found her constant chatter annoying. Still, her stories intrigued me.

I sat at a long table with all the books we'd need stacked neatly on the surface. I glanced up at the clock and winced. This is not a good look. At all.

At a quarter past, I saw her sauntering around bookshelves and waving hello to other students inside the library.

She made her way toward the table and sat across from me.

"How long have you been here?"

"Since 3:55," I said flatly.

She chuckled. "Who arrives right on time?"

"I do," I snapped.

She smiled, unaffected by my irritability, and opened her book.

I waited a beat and thought, I guess I better not hold my breath expecting an apology.

She launched into another information dump.

"I was planning on getting a coffee, then I changed my mind. I was almost here, then I changed it again. I drank it before I got here because it was a small cup."

I stared, in awe, at this rabid energy.

"I'm sorry I didn't get one for you. I thought about it afterward, but I was already late enough."

She looked up from her book to see me smiling wide.

"What's that look for?" She asked.

"I'm sorry. I just realized that I like how much you talk. It's... soothing? I'm not sure if that's the right word?"

The yellow and red undertones of her dark skin glowed as she tried to hold back a smile. She seemed to force a frown instead and focused on the assignment.

"When you live on the south side of Chicago, you have to do a lot of talking to be heard," she said matter-of-factly.

The look on my face pressed her for more details.

She read the cue.

"It's just that, there's always chaos. You are surrounded by noise, music, yelling, laughing..." she trailed off.

Her mind went somewhere, and I could see she was deep in thought. In an instant, she was back, talking a mile a minute.

"So basically, whenever I hear silence, I have to fill it."

I nodded slowly, processing what she had just told me.

"Anyway, you're not much of a talker, so I thought I should carry the weight."

I smiled at the jab.

"Maybe I don't talk much because *you* always have something to say?" I teased.

She rolled her eyes but laughed anyway.

"Just focus on the assignment," she said.

And so, it began.

We'd meet a few times a week, depending on our schedules. We settled on the library since it was convenient, quiet, and had enough room for all our research materials. Over time, it had become "our spot."

We even developed a pattern. I'd arrive on time, and to make up for the fact she was always late, she'd bring the coffee. On days she arrived on time, I supplied the caffeine jolt next time.

As the weeks passed, working with Alicen grew more enjoyable. I began to understand more about her and the loud personality that had somehow become endearing and familiar.

Her eyes sparkled whenever she talked about the bond she and her dad shared. She told me that after her brother died, he wanted to make sure she had everything she needed to survive. He taught her to think on her feet, trust no one, invest wisely, and never make decisions with her emotions. He didn't want her to be another victim.

I don't know why but getting to know Alicen stirred something inside me. I couldn't wait to see her. I hung on to her every word and even enjoyed our spirited debates. I felt comfortable around her. More than I have ever felt with any other woman. My feelings grew stronger the more time we spent together.

Honestly, I never thought I would consider dating someone of another race. I could kick myself for even saying this (albeit not out loud), but Alicen was different. I loved the color of her skin, but I wasn't consumed with it. She was so smart, complex, confident, and feisty as hell. All that mattered more to me than her melanin count.

Every time she sat next to me in class, my skin tingled. The way her hair smelled like a mix of vanilla and jasmine. It was intoxicating. I couldn't be near her for more than thirty seconds without my palms getting sweaty and my heart racing.

Thinking back, I've had several black friends, teammates, and shipmates, but none were female. I know I'm not a racist. Still, I could not make sense of why my feelings seemed unnatural. I heard my father's voice in the back of my mind, spouting racist rhetoric. I knew he was wrong. Alicen can't be blamed for the color of her skin. She had zero control over that!

We forged a friendship over time. She didn't have much interaction with people beyond her Chicago neighborhood. That's one of the reasons her parents wanted her to attend UK. They felt she needed to expand her horizons. They wanted her to challenge the perceived status quo.

The day we had to turn in our assignment, I read the paper over several times while eating breakfast, walking to class, sitting in my seat.

When Alicen arrived in class, she laughed and said, "I can see the steam coming out of your ears." She placed her hand over mine and gave it a tight squeeze.

My heart skipped a beat. I couldn't bring myself to look into her eyes. I didn't want her to see me blush.

"I just want this to be perfect," I said. "We worked so hard."

"And to think, you thought you would hate this class," she said.

"Do you want to go out afterward?" I asked.

I didn't recognize the person talking. It didn't sound like me. My words seemed forced; my voice nervous.

"We could get a burger at that place on campus you like."

My body tensed. Why was I still talking?

Her smile made me feel better.

"We deserve a break!" She exclaimed. "That was one of the hardest assignments, and school just started."

Two days later, we got our grades. An A.

We high-fived each other and stared at the paper, awestruck.

"Great job, guys," Dr. Sawyerr beamed.

"Thank you," we said in unison.

After class that day, I walked her to her dorm. When we approached her building, she stumbled, and the back of her hand brushed against mine. As we approached the dorm, a female voice called her name. We turned to see her roommate, Caitlyn, coming toward us. Caitlyn was as big as her social circle got.

"I've been looking for you, girl," she exclaimed in a heavy Brooklyn accent. Her thick hair flowed down her shoulders. She was short, curvy, and wore the tightest jeans and shirts imaginable.

"Who's this guy?" She asked the question as if I weren't standing right there.

"He's my partner, you know, the one from the class that I told you about," Alicen replied.

What was that I heard in her voice? Was that...joy? It was all I could do not to break out in the biggest smile.

Caitlyn crossed her arms and looked me up and down.

"How'd you do on your assignment?" She directed the question toward Alicen but kept her eyes on me. She didn't seem to trust me.

"We aced it!" Alicen exclaimed, interrupting the uncomfortable exchange.

Caitlyn nodded proudly.

"Yeah, ya did, girl! Not surprised!"

She pulled Alicen away to gossip about their classes.

"Well, that was awkward," I said under my breath.

In the days that followed, the three of us started spending our free time together. I'm not sure what transpired between her and Alicen when I left the afternoon we met, but Caitlyn became a bit more receptive. She still glared at me, and I imagined her praying I would just disappear. But I wasn't going to let her get in the way of the love of my life.

Yes, I said it. I was in love with Alicen, and no one would ruin that, especially not some catty roommate with an imaginary axe to grind.

One evening, I convinced Alicen to come out without Caitlyn. We walked around campus, discussing upcoming midterms. For the first time, I slipped my hand into hers. Our fingers intertwined. I held my breath and looked straight ahead, trying to be casual. Out of the corner of my eye, I saw her look up at me with a sly grin.

"It's about time," she said under her breath.

I smiled and leaned in to kiss her cheek. Just as I did, she turned her head towards me.

Our lips met, and I panicked. I almost pulled away, but she threw her arms around my neck. I cupped her face and began tracing her braids from root to end.

"Beautiful," I whispered.

I was lost in our embrace.

When she pulled away, I felt like a piece of me went with her. I wanted to taste the sweetness of her lips longer. I stared into her eyes.

After a brief silence, we smiled and kissed again.

That evening, we spoke on the phone all through the night. Luckily, we were on break from classes.

We went for breakfast the next day. Later that afternoon, I snuggled beside her on the common room couch. She rested her head on my chest and hugged me tightly. I never wanted to let her go. Even when she was right beside me, I ached for more. I wanted to know every detail about her life and dreams for the future. Spending every day with her was never enough. When she looked at me, I felt like I was home.

The most attractive thing about Alicen was her ability to think for herself, a gift she credits to her father.

One morning, I had no idea I would hear an opinion that would give me a glimpse into her thinking about a serious issue.

We approached a crowd of students. They were shouting and waving handmade signs, marching around a **rebel Civil War statue.**

As we got closer, we realized it was a student branch of **"Black Lives Matter."** I'd seen their protests on the news and saw posts on social media. Seeing it in person made it real.

Again, I heard my father's voice in my head, trying to push through and become relevant. What was he trying to tell me?

My heart raced, and I broke into a sweat.

Alicen seemed concerned about me. She led me to a nearby bench, and we sat there silently. I couldn't take my eyes off the protestors. **Their chants overpowered the voices in my head.**

"Are you okay?" she asked, handing me her water bottle.

I took it but couldn't drink. My eyes widened. My mouth had gone dry. "I'm fine," I said, voice cracking.

WHY SELL LIES WHEN THE TRUTH IS FREE

"I wonder if they even know why they're mad," Alicen said. "I hope they understand what could happen to them if they're not careful. They're protesting the small statue, but the largest rebel statue in America is right behind them. The media strikes again," she expressed with annoyance.

I turned my head and looked at Alicen. She was stone-faced, staring at the protesters.

"This is the ignorance my dad told me to look out for," she snarled. He'd say, **"When you fight, you better have a clear understanding of what you're fighting for."**

Her words pierced the air.

I didn't know it then, but we had just turned a critical corner in our relationship.

ADOLF RUPP

CHAPTER 5

"

To know what you know and what you do not know, that is true knowledge.

CONFUCIUS

F ortunately, she broke the silence. "My father was right," she said, almost whispering.

I hesitated, unsure of how to respond without making a mistake. Avoiding eye contact, I pondered the right course of action. I stood there, bewildered and afraid of offending her or asking an ignorant question. I didn't want to hurt her. Finally, I gathered the courage to ask, "What do you mean?"

It seemed like a safe question; one that wouldn't incite a civil war. I simply sought clarification. Alicen stared at me with an expression that shattered my heart and twisted my stomach.

I wanted to kick myself. Obviously, I did end up asking an inappropriate question. Where were the guidelines for discussing such sensitive matters?

"Why are they protesting and demanding to be heard in front of statues of these men?" she asked. It came off as a rhetorical question. Clearly, she already knew the answer.

"They are missing the point completely."

I, however, had no idea. The realization filled me with shame. My shoulders slumped. I didn't utter a word.

"It's no secret that in the early 1900s, states were enacting Jim Crow laws to disenfranchise Black Americans," she explained.

"They erected these statues to legitimize white supremacy. Why would anyone put up a Robert E. Lee or Stonewall Jackson statue in Baltimore in 1948?"

I was stunned. Despite understanding every word Alicen said, I was still confused about why she didn't agree with the protesters. I did admire how eloquently she expressed the frustrations of African Americans. Still, I couldn't fully grasp the point she was trying to make.

"It's not that I don't agree," she sighed, undoubtedly sensing my confusion.

"Look to your left," she prompted.

I turned, but all I saw were the hallowed grounds where our proud Kentucky Wildcats basketball team played.

"I'm confused," I finally admitted out loud. My cheeks burn with embarrassment.

"Do you know who the gymnasium is named after?" she asked.

"Adolf Rupp," I replied, proud I could contribute something factual to the conversation.

"Correct," she nodded firmly. "What do you know about Rupp?"

I smiled and responded confidently.

"He won 876 games in forty-one years of coaching at the University of Kentucky. It's impossible to grow up in Kentucky and not know his story. Every kid hears about it at least once in their lifetime."

I searched her face for approval.

Alicen pursed her lips, her eyes reflecting a mix of emotions.

"He's also the same person who proudly proclaimed that black basketball players weren't mentally equipped to compete with white players," she retorted.

"Yeah, but..."

I tried to counter with more facts, but she was way ahead of me.

"Sure, he later recruited Black players in his career, but only after the all-black starting lineup defeated his 'superior' Wildcat squad in the 1966 NCAA Championship."

She sneered at the word "superior." I stared at her, rendered speechless by her words.

"What puzzles me is why Black parents across the nation pray for their sons or daughters to play in this arena. It literally is the biggest rebel statue in America. The Stonewall statue is bad, but as we do so often (she pointed at the back of her hand), we ignore the bigger problem."

It was starting to sink in.

"They are focusing on a small piece of an issue and blowing past the big picture."

Clarity.

I wondered how Coach Rupp would feel about the predominantly Black squads that had taken the court for Kentucky for over twenty years.

Scratching my head, I mustered the courage to ask, "Why would you want to attend this school if you feel this way?"

She looked at me, her gaze penetrating and unsettling. Had I said something wrong? Was she angry with me? I couldn't decipher her emotions.

"That's not the issue," she said softly, taking my hand as we walked. "My father insisted I attend because they offered me a full scholarship. It's his way of seeking long-overdue reparations. He made it clear not a single penny of his money would contribute to the perpetuation of this institution."

My jaw dropped.

"So, you don't have any expenses? Not even toiletries? That's impressive."

She brushed off my comment. She seemed conflicted.

"I mean, sometimes we make decisions that don't align with our views," I offered. "No judgment," I teased.

She was not amused.

We walked in silence, drawing nearer to her dorm. Excitement about the new chapter in our relationship rippled through me. Our conversation could have become divisive, but I learned more about her instead.

"I still think Coach Rupp was one of the greatest coaches in NCAA history," I said cautiously, hoping not to stir up trouble.

"I agree," she replied, catching me off guard. **"The frustration lies in the fact the entire story isn't told. I know it's a lot for you to take in, but it goes so much deeper for me. And this is not the first time I've had to unpack this misconception...no, wait...misrepresentation!"**

This was so overwhelming, but I wanted (no, needed) to know more. I was probably a glutton for punishment because this wasn't the easiest conversation. However, the passion in her voice had me mesmerized. Her pain was visceral, and in that moment, I would have done anything to make her feel better, to give her peace.

Maybe I was, by just listening and not judging.

"What else affected you deeply, if you don't mind my asking?"

"No, I don't mind at all. I appreciate it, actually."

I smiled, stood straight up, and motioned as if I was zipping my lips, a sign that she had my rapt attention.

Remember the movie "Roots," by Alex Hailey?

"Vaguely. He was the guy who wrote the book about tracing his ancestors back to slavery, right?"

"Well, sort of," she replied.

I settled in for what clearly was going to be one hell of a revelation.

"I'll never forget when I found out the truth about Hailey," she said painfully.

"I won't lie, and I am not exaggerating when I tell you the real story about him devastated me. It was as if something had ripped away a part of my identity, leaving me questioning everything I thought I knew about my history as an African American."

I didn't dare interrupt.

"That dude was celebrated for that book. He claimed he was telling the story of his ancestors' journey from Gambia to slavery in America."

She inhaled deeply, as if she was remembering the story for the first time. I moved closer, not wanting to miss a single word.

"Man, that story resonated with me, my parents...an entire community! We had never seen this portrayal of the struggles and resilience of African Americans throughout history. We'd heard about it, of course, and if you had the right people around

you, read documented history that I can assure you was not readily available. But to see it…"

I mouthed the words silently after she said them…

"But to see it," I parroted.

"Marty, don't you know, a few years ago, while I was having a random conversation with a Black historian, the truth began to unravel?"

I was struck by the sound of my name coming out of her beautiful mouth.

Focus, man… don't mess this up, I thought!

"There was this big copyright lawsuit. Two, as a matter of fact. When I started researching the story, I read an article in *The Times of London*. I think…"

She paused as if to confirm the Times was indeed the source. She probably didn't want to add to any misinformation."

"The journalist launched an investigation, raising even more questions about the factual basis of the African portion of Hailey's account. It just got worse after that. The authenticity of the narrative started to deteriorate."

I could *feel* her heart racing, if that was even possible!

"Hailey finally admitted parts of "Roots" were fiction, but he denied knowingly making any factual errors, blah, blah, blah."

I resisted the urge to laugh. Alicen can be very dry and witty without even trying.

"He defended the book as a symbolic history, a representation of the experiences of a people," she continued. "But the damage was done. In fact, I think they proved at least three passages in his book were lifted from an earlier work titled "The African.""

"Dam," was all I could manage.

"The more I learned, the more I questioned if my own heritage was based on a lie?"

I could tell this was a devastating blow. Her face said it all. Her heart ached with what I could only describe as a profound sense of betrayal.

"To this day, I tell this story to anyone who even tries to make Hailey sound like some kind of ancestral hero. Nope. He ain't! And believe it or not, folks will try to justify it or insist the truth was not the truth!"

I felt that. I hated it when people tried to convince me that what I know I know, can't be right.

"I know this is more than you probably signed up for," she said, laughing softly.

"It's just when unfavorable aspects of prominent figures are revealed, people look at them differently. In Hailey's case, that is absolutely appropriate! Screw that liar!"

Well, safe to say she really had no love lost for that guy!

"As for Rupp, sure, he can be considered one of the greats. But that doesn't mean he did not harbor biases against Black players. I mean, if we're going to keep it honest, it was part of the era he lived in."

"So, what do you think is the deal behind Rupp? Why are people in some kind of denial?"

"People fear it will tarnish his legacy if the truth comes out, but that doesn't diminish his impressive record. The two are mutually exclusive."

"So, you admire him a little, then?" I inquired.

She shrugged; a gesture filled with ambivalence.

"I can't say I like or dislike someone I've never met. I can't ignore the numbers, though; they clearly show he was a legendary coach in NCAA basketball."

"That's one way to see it," I said, appreciating her willingness to share her perspective.

"As for me, I can only go by what I've been told, and in this Bluegrass state, Coach Rupp could do no wrong. My father would list a ton of reasons not to cheer for the Wildcats. At some point, I think he regretted things were not like they used to be. Maybe he longed to relive those days."

"My aunt Alice has a basketball story you should hear. Hopefully, you'll have the pleasure of meeting her. She can shed a lot more light on the past."

"So, you're named after her?"

"Yep. I'm a lot like her, too."

Alicen squeezed my hand and kissed my cheek.

We finally reached her dormitory. I watched her ascend the steps, admiring her from afar.

"Goodnight," I shouted, disappointed the night was ending.

I made my way to my dorm, feeling good about the love story that was developing between us.

PROUD HAITIAN GIRL

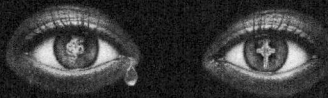

CHAPTER 6

"

It is easy to hate, and it is difficult to love. This is how the whole scheme of things works. All good things are difficult to achieve; and bad things are very easy to get.

CONFUCIUS

My four years of college were a whirlwind, filled with surprises, challenges, and countless opportunities to meet people from all walks of life. I thought I had seen and encountered it all in the Navy, but the University of Kentucky surpassed my experiences in more ways than I could have imagined.

I felt so accomplished. I set my mind on getting a degree, and I did it. Many of my friends had set lofty goals, and I watched them give up, one at a time. I'm not sure if I had something to prove, but this was one dream I would realize by any means. Between taking classes, making sure I had enough credits each semester to graduate on time and building my relationship with Alicen, I felt academics and passion collide. I was thankful that friendships were forged amid the chaos of exams and late-night study sessions.

My perspective on the world expanded in college. I became acutely aware of the racial tensions that simmered beneath the surface, especially on campus. Conversations with Alicen and her friends forced me to confront the uncomfortable truths about the **history of Black people in America**. I realized that the narratives I had been taught were often tainted by false depictions and missing pieces of the past. The painful reality sank in and ignited a fire inside me. I became determined to always vet what I heard, ask questions, challenge perspectives, seek the truth, and ensure I always understood what or whom I was defending. I have Alicen to thank for that.

Alicen proved to be, without a doubt, the most interesting person I had the pleasure of meeting. With every disagreement, I learned something new. Even if we were not on the same page, I had to give her credit. She knew her stuff. From her choice of major to the sheer drive she displayed in every aspect of her life, that woman was determined to graduate with a psychology degree.

We always went back to one of the most painful experiences in her life, losing her brother to gun violence. It was a reality that punctuated every decision she seemed to make academically.

She was convinced that a mental health crisis played a significant role in driving violence, especially in underserved communities. All she wanted to do was return home and play a role in changing all that.

I spent the last few weeks reflecting on my time at UK. Turns out, it was not a microcosm of the diverse tapestry of humanity. However, it did bring people from different backgrounds, cultures, and perspectives to one campus. I met individuals who **shattered stereotypes**, challenged preconceived notions, and inspired me with their resilience.

I didn't go off the deep end by developing some wide-eyed, rose-colored lens view of life. I learned there was value in embracing our differences. I even witnessed the power of unity when faced with hatred and adversity.

Ultimately, I accepted people were more alike than they cared to admit, and folks shared many experiences that transcended the boundaries of race, religion, or nationality.

I also faced frustrating realities. **The shadow of prejudice and discrimination still penetrated the confines of a supposedly enlightened institution.**

Witnessing the subtle biases was disheartening; some days, you could slice through the underlying tensions with a knife. Still, **my relationship with Alicen stood as a testament to the possibility of transcending those barriers**, of finding solace and strength in the arms of someone whose heart saw beyond skin color.

Together, we navigated the drama of academia, supporting each other through sleepless nights and endless essays.

She challenged me to think critically, question assumptions, and embrace the uncomfortable conversations at the heart of self-reflection and growth.

Our time alone would have been perfect were it not for Alicen's roommate, Caitlyn, hanging around us like a plague...with an attitude. If I didn't know any better, I would think they were in a relationship (or maybe Caitlyn wished they were). Everything was a competition. Whenever I bought Alicen a birthday gift, Caitlyn made it her mission to outdo me. I seriously did not understand why she despised me so much. Hell, if she wasn't so toxic, I'd really like her.

Caitlyn was a proud Haitian girl. Not that she hated America, she just had an intense love for the country and sang the praises of her culture in every way. The woman celebrated Haitian Flag Day religiously and went all out for Haitian Independence Day. She even found a remote restaurant a few miles from campus that prepared the traditional pumpkin soup that marked the occasion. Caitlyn and I didn't get along most of the time, but I made nice when she had the soup around. It was really good!

Her parents taught her that the Haiti media chose to portray was not the country they knew. Yes, there was extreme poverty and corrupt politics, and the country has yet to recover from the catastrophic natural disasters that claimed hundreds of thousands of lives in the last decade. However, parts of the country still rivaled any Caribbean paradise.

Haiti has produced renowned physicians, engineers, educators, scientists, and artists. From food to arts to science, the country has played a critical role in America's past and present.

Having met her parents a few times, I figured out their personalities. Her father seemed submissive, but he was actually quite opinionated. Her mother was a force to be reckoned with. Caitlyn seemed to align more with her mother's character.

Some days, when I watched them interact, I'd think no wonder she was so intense. She probably has trouble identifying who she really is, and she projects all that confusion onto me.

Or she's just a bitch, plain and simple.

Alicen's father, Serge, was also a character. He was a proud union man who had no reservations about making his views known. He reminded me of my late father (not in a good way). His thinking was one-sided. On top of that, he identified as a Republican, which blew my mind. He'd often say that the **Democratic Party ruined the Black community with handouts**. Mr. Reynolds delivered the assertion with such bluster and disgust it made me uncomfortable. I never knew how to react. I kept my thoughts to myself.

I mean, what do you even say to something like that?

If I had to sum up my time at UK, I'd say it gave me more than just a degree. It gave me a deeper understanding of the world.

What I thought would last an eternity went by so fast that it seemed as if I didn't have enough time to enjoy it. Phase two of my adult journey ended. We were one week from graduation. Time flies when you're having fun; the last four years were just that.

I stood on the precipice of graduation, and I reflected on the transformative journey I had undertaken. It was a passage that led me to the love of my life, transformed me into an advocate for truth and justice, and inspired me to break down barriers that hinder the progress of our society.

With a grateful heart, I couldn't wait for the moment I stepped off the stage, diploma in hand, and embraced the next chapter of my life.

Finally, the big day arrived. Commencement. I could barely contain my excitement!

My mom drove up with my brother. I visited more frequently over the years and saw the toll caring for him took on my mother as she got older. The weight of my father's absence aged her prematurely. **However, she balked any time I suggested placing my brother in a 24-hour care facility.** My mother pleaded with me and made me promise I would never put my brother in a home.

I gave her my word.

When they called my name, I walked across the stage with pride, accepting my passport to the next phase of adulthood—the degree that symbolized a key to navigating society. But unlike the military training that readied me for survival, college felt like uncharted territory.

After the ceremony, Alicen went to dinner with Caitlyn and her parents. I spent time with my mom and Lance.

It was time to go back home and continue my life.

Who knew that the grand finale of my college experience would lead to a revelation; one that would test the strength of the love that had blossomed within the hallowed halls of the University of Kentucky.

UNION PACIFIC RAILROAD

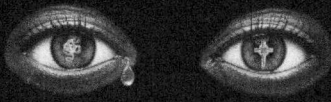

CHAPTER 7

"

We're born alone, we live alone, we die alone. Only through our love and friendship can we create the illusion for the moment that we're not alone.

ORSON WELLES

Graduation had come and gone. I finally came down off my celebration high and found myself back home in Paducah, Kentucky, with my mother and Lance. The post-college reality hit hard. I struggled to find employment in a job market that seemed to shrink daily. Amid the uncertainty, one constant kept my spirits afloat—Alicen.

She returned to Chicago. I made frequent trips there, and she came to Paducah occasionally. We decided it made more sense for me to travel to her because I was still unemployed. Not to mention, Chitown had a much better nightlife for young adults.

Alicen was consumed by a desire to make a difference. She wanted to contribute to the healing and restoration of a city marred by brokenness. It did not surprise me when she landed a job at a mental health facility, a perfect fit for her compassionate nature. Alicen firmly believed that society often failed to understand and notice and (unfortunately) neglected people like her and those she wanted to help.

Alicen's brother was a victim of senseless gun violence. That really fueled her dedication. She established a connection between his death and the alarming rise of black-on-black murders in Chicago, and she wanted the world to see it, too.

While I admired her unwavering passion, I must confess that I had never fully grasped the depth of her perspective until now.

The distance between us took its toll, and I realized how much I missed her. Our connection was more than just words; it was an unspoken understanding that transcended physical presence. Being apart meant not having that person to confide in, to share every thought and emotion with. The ache of missing her grew with each passing day. Although she visited occasionally, and I made trips to Chicago, it never felt like enough. The yearning in my heart intensified, and I longed for a resolution that would bring us closer together once and for all.

As I settled back home, I watched my mother tirelessly care for my brother, shouldering the responsibility with unwavering love and dedication. Deep down, I felt obligated to ease some of the burden. My brother had matured during my absence, assisting Mom with daily chores and adapting well to a structured routine. Still, the weight of his care rested heavily on her, and I couldn't help but feel I should contribute more to his well-being.

One day, Alicen called, brimming with excitement. I sensed she had something significant to share, and it piqued my curiosity. She had told me countless stories about her uncle, a mysterious figure tucked away upstairs at her grandmother's house, whom she had never known until recently. Uncle Mike held a special place in Alicen's heart, emerging as her favorite person.

Alicen said Uncle Mike believed he could secure a job for me.

"Nothing is guaranteed yet, but Uncle Mike thinks he can pull some strings," she said.

"Wait. What's the job?"

"Well, before I tell you, I have to ask... are you willing to move here?"

I had asked myself the same question at the end of each visit. I wished for the day that goodbyes would end; no more collecting frequent flyer miles. I never imagined her moving here, so if we were to become one, it would be in Chicago, not my quiet hometown.

Before I could fill my mind with another thought, I enthusiastically replied, "Yes! Now, what's the job?"

The job description puzzled me. Terminal manager for Union Pacific Railroad. Trains were foreign territory to me. I voiced my concerns to Alicen. She reassured me that her uncle guaranteed they would provide the training. I would attend a six-week school in Omaha before receiving my permanent assignment in Chicago. It all sounded surreal, a leap into the unknown.

Before fully embracing the opportunity, I knew I had to discuss it with my mother. Alicen's uncle held the key to a job opportunity that could change my life, but it meant leaving behind the two people who meant the world to me. The weight of responsibility hung heavy in the air, intertwining with the anticipation of a brighter future. In the coming days, I would have to face the ultimate crossroad, a choice that would shape my path and the lives of those I held closest to my heart.

I found my mom in the kitchen, busy preparing lunch. I opened up about my concerns regarding the lack of employment in our small town and my diminishing savings. I didn't want to burden her further, especially knowing how much she had already endured.

She looked into my eyes, a mixture of wisdom and love shining through. At that moment, it felt as though she could read my mind. She reassured me I had never been a burden and that she had weathered storms far worse. And then she uttered words that struck a chord within me—words that echoed her unspoken understanding of my dreams and desires.

"Son, mothers always know. Alicen is a remarkable woman; you shouldn't let her slip away. Your life has never truly been here since you swore into the Navy. Your dreams are too big, and your potential is too bright to wither away in this town. Go out there and live your dreams. I'll always be here, supporting you every step of the way."

Her words resounded deeply within me, instilling a sense of purpose and validation. It was as if she had given me her blessing to chase after the life I desired. But with her unwavering support came a realization that struck a pang of guilt within me—the prospect of leaving her behind to shoulder the burden of caring for my brother.

LOVE IS STRONGER THAN HATE

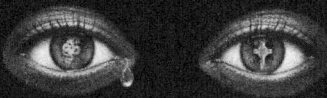

CHAPTER 8

"

The only thing
new in the world
is the history you
do not know.

HARRY S. TRUMAN

S ix months flew by. Besides the unpredictable schedule, work was going well. However, I did not know how complex managing a rail terminal would be. It's a whirlwind of activity and responsibility. Every day, I oversee the makeup and breakup of trains. It's a jigsaw puzzle of cars, each fitting into its designated place.

I spend hours reviewing train schedules and switching orders, examining timetables, mapping out the movement of trains throughout the terminal, ensuring that trains arrive and depart on time, and maximizing efficiency while maintaining safety.

It's a delicate balance,

Yard switching is serious business. I orchestrate the movement of trains from track to track, carefully maneuvering them to their designated locations. It requires precision and attention to detail, as the slightest miscalculation can cause major delays or disruptions.

Despite the chaos, there is a sense of satisfaction that comes with overseeing the terminal's operations. It's a job that requires both technical expertise and a passion for the railway industry, a passion that I can honestly say was growing. **This was a far cry from my childhood memories.** I remember trains passing by. I waved, and if the engineer was cool, he'd blow the horn. I wish they knew how much that makes a child's day. I would be in my glory.

I get to re-experience that feeling when I conduct elementary school tours when the schedule allows. I don't know who gets the most out of them, the kids or the administrators. Either way, it feels good to be the reason they smile.

I marveled at my good fortune. Here I am, at this transformative phase in my life, with a great salary, a job I love, and the woman of my dreams. This must be what heaven feels like. **As my professional life evolved, I contemplated another big decision.**

For years, I had been waiting for the perfect moment to propose to the love of my life. We created a journey together that was filled with laughter, support, love, and countless shared memories. Her family embraced me with open arms. Well, everyone but her dad. He never hid his disdain. I knew he had nothing against me personally. He had an issue with his daughter dating a white man, no matter how nice that white man was.

Most of her family saw the love we shared, and it brought them joy. My family felt the same. My mother adored Alicen. She saw the light in her eyes and the kindness in her heart. My brother, who had always looked up to me, admired Alicen. No doubt he sensed her strength, intelligence, and compassion. Some things can penetrate the limited cognitive function of mental disability.

Seeing how seamlessly she had become a part of my family deepened my love for her.

I couldn't imagine my life without her. I pictured my racist father turning in his grave at the thought of his son falling in love with a woman of a different race. **But my love for Alicen was stronger than any prejudice, and I was ready to face whatever challenges lay ahead.**

I was eager to take that leap of faith and ask her to be my partner for life, my equal, my forever. I saved up for months with a singular purpose: buy a ring befitting the amazing woman she is.

Now, all I have to do is muster enough courage to ask her father for her hand in marriage. Alicen and I had remained respectful of her strict, religious upbringing and had not moved in together. Occasionally, she stayed overnight. I'm sure that was a discussion she did not have with her parents.

Her father and I had our disagreements. From restaurants to movies, right down to music. He enjoyed Country and Western music. I hated it. In his mind, it was the last real music left. In my mind, I'd be perfectly happy if I never heard another whiny twang. I was more of a Jay-Z, Drake, and Kanye West guy. He despised them. He felt they misled the youth with their lyrics and forced kids to lose sight of the struggle with their message.

"You can't blame Drake," I'd say. "He's just a Jewish kid from the suburbs of Toronto trying to fit into his father's world."

"He should know by now the grass is not always greener on the other side," he'd retort.

I just let it go. It was not worth the aggravation to debate the finer points of hip-hop with this man.

Still, in some odd way, I enjoyed some of our conversations (even though he talked at me instead of to me). I always learned something. I heard the frustrations of a **Black man carrying years of anger for several reasons.** To be honest, sometimes I wondered if he knew exactly why he was so angry. The thought always took me back to the first time I heard Alicen voice her frustration with the protestors at UK. She wondered if they even knew what they were speaking out against. How ironic that I was asking the same question about her father all these years later!

He reminded me of my father. **He was the George Jefferson to my father's Archie Bunker.**

Man, Norman Lear was so ahead of his time.

I chose a Saturday spring morning. I went over my speech one hundred times in the mirror. I have never felt a good vibe from him. A part of me says no matter what his answer is, she will make up her own mind. Alicen was stubborn, just like him.

"What's the worst that can happen?" I asked myself as I pulled up to her house.

We had planned a golf outing. We even gave the occasion a name. **"Guy time on the back nine."** He loved golfing. It was one of the few occasions he seemed to like me. I figured this would be the best time to ask for his blessing.

We made our way to the country club, where he was a member for over 20 years. I know this because he reminded me every chance he got. We played a round and joked and made some small talk. My stomach was in knots the entire time.

As we returned to the club, I practiced my pitch silently one last time.

The valet took his time bringing the car. At one point, I wanted to say forget it and wait for the next time I mustered up the courage. When the valet finally pulled up to the entrance, got out, and handed him the keys, I knew the moment of truth had arrived.

We drove in silence for about three miles. I cleared my throat. He looked at me, slightly annoyed. Finally, I spoke.

"Mr. Reynolds, can I ask you a question?"

"No! I still don't like the Kentucky Wildcats. I don't care who the new coach is."

We chuckled.

"No, sir, not that. It's about Alicen."

That comment let the air out of the car. He set his jaw as if expecting the worst. Instinctively, I felt for the ring in my pocket. I'd forgotten everything I wanted to say.

"What about Alicen?"

"I would like to ask you for her hand in marriage."

"Are you crazy, boy?" He barked.

I tensed up.

"Let me first say, no. Actually…hell no!

I sat motionless, stunned.

"Let me explain something to you, boy."

I thought he had one more "boy" before I went off.

"You are a fine young man with a bright future. I have nothing against you, but I love my daughter and have always done everything I can to protect her. That *includes* **shielding her from all the problems that will come with being in an interracial marriage."**

This was not going as planned. I expected Mr. Renolds to be somewhat hesitant, but this was downright brutal.

"And before you start blabbing about how it's different today, tell that to the people in Charlottesville, Virginia. Better yet, how about we ride to Texas and talk to the family of the late James Byrd, Jr.?"

We discussed these tragedies often, and I thought I'd convinced him I agreed with his stance. Now, he was using these atrocities to attack me and my love for his daughter. I felt the blood drain from my face.

He was just getting started.

"I'm not saying all white people are racist, but there are enough of them around to cause trouble for no reason. I still have memories of growing up in Hattiesburg, Mississippi, where the Ku Klux Klan attacked the home of NAACP leader Vernon Dahmer with firebombs and gunfire, all because they didn't want us to vote or have equal rights. Young man, that was not long ago. Some laws may have changed, but it's like putting a Band-Aid on a bullet wound."

This hostility was more than I could stand. I gritted my teeth, clenched my jaw, and hid my balled-up fists in my lap. As much as I wanted to lash out at him, he was still Alicen's father. Nothing good would come of being disrespectful. I just had to sit there and take it.

"I don't know what you are thinking. It was just 1960 when Leona Tate had to be escorted to schools by U.S. Marshalls because white people did not want her there, and in 1970, when Alicen's aunt, Alice Hunt, was good enough to score a game-winning shot but not good enough to dine in a restaurant with her team. Do you get my point, son?"

This history lesson on race and oppression was going too far, and he was missing the point completely!

"But I love your daughter with all my heart," I sputtered pitifully.

"*Love?*" he scoffed.

"You think love will solve these problems you guys will face? That your children, Lord forbid you have any, will face? Did you think this out? This is not a movie, son. This is real life."

I was numb.

"So, hell no," he repeated as if saying it the first time was not enough.

The rest of the ride home was tense, to say the least. The silence was deafening, and my heart was shattered.

Alicen and her mom were surprised we got back so early. We were usually gone until after lunch. Unaware of the gaping chasm that had formed between their vitriolic patriarch and me, they prattled on about some popular healthy eating documentary on Netflix. I expected Alicen would sanction some strict dietary restrictions when we got married. I could already hear her saying, "If it were not for the genius marketing of Leo Barnett, America would have never been so addicted to beef."

I would have loved to entertain the debate, but I didn't have the emotional energy. Alicen could tell right away that something was not right.

As her dad walked past his favorite chair and made a B-line for the bedroom, she and I locked eyes.

WINDS OF UNCERTAINTY

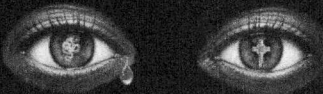

CHAPTER 9

"

Your word is the only thing you can give and keep at the same time.

AARON LEE WALLACE JR.

was trapped in an awful nightmare, one from which I desperately wanted to wake up. It reminded me of the night terrors I used to experience my first week in boot camp, except this time, I knew it was real, and I hated being wide awake.

My life overflowed with peace and boundless love twenty-four hours ago. When I prepared to ask Mr. Reynolds for Alicen's hand in marriage, I steadied myself, asking, **"What's the worst that could happen?"** I never fathomed this cataclysmic blow.

I kept replaying the experience in my head, and it got worse every time. The brutal, insensitive tone of his voice still reverberated in my ears, his words echoing through the chambers of my shattered heart. I consider myself thick-skinned and not too easily offended or otherwise affected by what someone says to me. This time, devastation consumed me. Mostly because there was so much at stake. He stood between me and my future. It was so surreal.

Alicen knew me very well. She had only to size me up for a few seconds to see the anguish on my face as we stood outside her home.

She walked me to my car and asked, her voice trembling with concern, "Marty, what's wrong?"

Her eyes were filled with tenderness and worry (and a touch of annoyance because she didn't have much patience for dramatic emotional displays). She waited for answers.

I couldn't summon the strength to tell her the truth. I was concerned about her response and didn't want to see her have a meltdown. The silence was heavy. Finally, I kissed Alicen on the forehead and promised to call when I got home.

"So, we'll talk then?"

I smiled faintly and said, "We'll see, babe. I'm kind of tired, so I may just head right to bed. I love you."

"I love you too," she replied, her voice full of disappointment.

The ride home seemed longer than usual. My desire to call my mother and seek her comfort grew stronger each mile. It reminded me of the countless times I sought her love in moments of frustration.

Echoes of past setbacks returned.

This time, there was no one to confide in. Alicen had become my only sounding board. I wouldn't dream of sharing the intimate aspects of our relationship with anyone else. I had a few good friends, some I'd known since we were kids, but she was the only person I trusted completely, the only person whose opinion I truly valued.

That was part of the reason I loved her so much. There was little I could not share with her. Even if it pissed her off, she could at least listen and do her best to understand. How ironic; I was carrying one of the greatest burdens I've faced since meeting her, and for the first time in a long time, I was afraid to open up to her, the woman I wanted to marry.

How could I bear this problem alone?

When I got home, I sent Alicen a text, feigning composure. I let her know I made it safe and wanted to go right to bed. She persisted, begging me to call her.

Words eluded me.

I did the unthinkable: I lied to her. I made up a story about an emergency at work, explaining that a manager wanted me to come in on my day off. Recognizing my dilemma (or so I thought), Alicen reluctantly ended our text exchange.

Days drifted by, and not much changed. I hid behind uncomfortable walls of silence on the issue. We exchanged the customary "I love you," "I miss you," and "can't wait to see you" texts, clinging to fragments of affection. And then, a seismic shift occurred within our digital exchanges.

"Can't wait to see you" became "I can't wait to become Mrs. Ruane."

I froze, a torrent of emotions cascading over me. Now, I heard about this so-called woman's intuition, and, at this moment, it felt undeniably real. Did her father mention it? Had he tried to make his case about why we shouldn't marry? I panicked, thinking this guy had turned into some kind of relationship terrorist!

Curiosity got the best of me. I called her. My heart was pounding.

She answered, her voice was subdued.

"What made you say that?" I asked, my voice trembling.

"I don't know," she replied, a trace of uncertainty lacing her words. "I was at work, and a coworker announced her engagement over the weekend. It made me feel a way."

Her answer crushed my spirit even further. That announcement should have been ours. Her father had robbed us both of this moment. I found myself incapable of mirroring the earnestness in her voice.

Finally, she broke the silence.

"Are you busy, babe? I can let you go."

"No, it's not that," I confessed, my voice heavy. "I have to tell you something, but first, promise me you won't get upset."

"I can't make that promise," she responded honestly. "But I'll do my best to contain any anger. Is that fair?"

"Yes," I whispered, bracing myself. "I wanted to ask you to marry me on Saturday, but your father said no."

Her tone shifted, a mixture of disbelief and defiance.

"My father? Marty, did you plan to propose to him or me?"

"Well, you, of course," I replied, a touch of frustration seeping into my voice. I wasn't in the mood for Mr. Reynolds 2.0. Now was not the time for pointed sarcasm.

"I wanted to be respectful and ask his permission," I explained.

Her voice softened. She replied carefully, "I hate to tell you this, but my dad will never deem any man worthy. He told me that right after I won the spelling bee in the third grade. My classmate Michael O'Brien came over to hug me, and Dad damn near stiff-armed the kid! It's nothing against you personally. He simply prefers that I never leave home."

I relaxed for the first time in days.

"So...do you want to try again?" she asked.

My heart soared, but I felt I had to be completely honest with her about my conversation with her father.

"Well...it wasn't just a no," I confessed, my voice marked with a bitterness I could not hide. "He was downright racist, Al, claiming that our union would be devoid of peace because of our racial differences. I swear, if I closed my eyes, I would have sworn those hateful comments were coming out of my father's mouth."

For a second, I thought she might have hung up.

"Hello, you there?" I asked, praying that was not the case.

She exhaled and, in the most confident, assured, straightforward way, replied, "Marty, I love and respect my father. He is strong-willed, diligent, and smart, and he has made a lot of his life despite obstacles.

I didn't know where this was going, but it didn't seem like she was exactly angry at her dad.

She continued, "**My dad is also stubborn and self-centered. I can't change that; I even understand why he is the way he is. But that's him. I refuse to let his prejudices dictate my happiness.**"

I shot straight up from the bed and started fighting the air, barely able to contain my happiness.

"So, you're saying..."

"The answer is yes!" Alicen proclaimed. "I love you more deeply than anyone I have ever loved. This may sound a little messed up, but that includes my father.

From then on, I promised myself that I would never have a day I didn't open up to Alicen. I was marrying my best friend, and she would become my most cherished (and my only) family. Of course, I had my mom and brother, but she and I would have a bond that transcended my relationship with them.

We began planning our wedding immediately.

Later that year, **we stood hand in hand, exchanging vows** in a small ceremony in the embrace of one of our favorite cities, New York. **Our dream wedding unfolded before us**, a celebration of love and resilience. **The majestic Cloisters, perched along the banks of the Hudson River**, was the perfect background for our ceremony. The **restaurant next to the Cloisters provided an exquisite location** for our tiny reception.

Alicen's father refused to attend the ceremony. I knew his rebuff was a terrible blow to her. Still, **she remained joyful,** refusing to let his obstinacy dampen the occasion.

Meanwhile, my mother introduced a woman as my aunt, which left me confused. This woman was literally a complete stranger. I don't even recall seeing her in pictures. I am positive my mother never shared a single story about this "sister." However, I didn't have the time or patience to deal with the unexpected revelation. I avoided anything that could ruin our wedding day.

For tonight, she was a welcome "relative".

Alicen graced the aisle in her mother's wedding gown, a timeless heirloom slightly altered to fit her perfectly. As her "something borrowed," she wore my mother's cherished diamond pendant, a symbol of two families intertwining.

My brother Lance, who had been showing so much progress and maturity as he managed his autism, was my best man. Alicen mentioned that his innocent affection veered into uncomfortable territory during their dance. She admitted she was a little taken aback by the encounter but immediately recognized that his actions stemmed from a lack of understanding. She showed grace and understanding, attributing the incident to Lance's condition.

Leave it to her to give me even more reasons to adore her.

As we celebrated our special day, the Pastor's sermon replayed in my head.

"Wherefore they are no more twain, but one flesh. What therefore God hath joined together, let not man put asunder."

I knew that was the pivotal moment: our promise before God that nothing and no one will ever come between us. I nearly cried; the words moved me so deeply. I think Alicen felt the same.

We enjoyed the day to the fullest.

As we reveled in our newfound union, the winds of uncertainty whispered in the background. We were about to face serious challenges.

Problems would start after I asked my mom about this "aunt" I knew nothing about.

Our story continued to unfold in unexpected ways.

SOUL OF HAITI

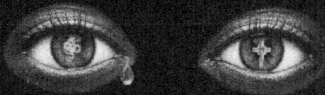

CHAPTER 10

"

History, in general, only informs us what bad government is.

THOMAS JEFFERSON

As the night drew to a close, our family wished us well. We limited the guest list to immediate family, but they heaped on the love and support! I was pleasantly surprised at the perfect harmony.

Caitlin and I set aside our differences and forged a new connection. She confided in me, peeling back the layers to reveal why her attitude toward me during college was so hateful. She feared I was nothing more than a passing fancy in Alicen's life. She was concerned I would eventually hurt her when we went our separate ways. I didn't know it back then, but Caitlin knew the depth of Alicen's love for me long before I understood it.

Throughout the celebration, she acknowledged her doubts were unfounded and delighted in our marital bliss.

We partied, we laughed, we cried, and Alicen and I thoroughly enjoyed what we knew would be one of the most memorable occasions in our new life together.

We checked into our hotel at about 11:00 p.m., packed, and settled into bed. We shared our favorite stories from our amazing wedding day.

We had to be at the airport early, but we were hopped up on adrenaline and happiness. We made love into the early morning hours, exploring each other like it was our first time together.

Our next adventure was about to begin!

The honeymoon was epic!

We followed Caitlin's recommendation and traveled to Jacmel; a charming port town nestled along the picturesque south coast of Haiti. Caitlin painted vivid pictures of the region, sharing stories of summers spent visiting her grandparents in this vibrant country. Her eyes sparkled with pride as she animatedly described the grandeur of the annual Carnival celebrations, flavorful foods, island spices, deep, crystal blue waters, and nights spent sipping the 5-star Rhum Barbancourt the country is known for! They describe the famous spirits in the amber brown bottle as the "soul of Haiti." Alicen and I had never tasted a rhum so smooth! And neither of us has ever been a big drinker! Still, we stocked up on a whole lot of that Haitian soul ahead of our trip back home!

I couldn't help but fall head over heels in love with Haiti, embracing its rich history and heritage. The things you learn when you are not locked into dormant thinking! The story of the Haitian people blew my mind. Even Alicen, who was much more versed in the history of struggle and redemption among people of color, was moved to tears at the sheer grandeur of this culture!

It was in Haiti that the first free Black republic in the world emerged following a bold revolution in 1804 against French colonial rule. We learned this was the only slave uprising that led to the founding of a state that was both free from slavery and ruled by non-whites and former captives. Our guide talked proudly about **Toussaint Louverture**, a free black, and one of the most celebrated revolutionary leaders of the Haitian Revolution, and Jean-Jacques Dessalines, a Haitian revolutionary and the first ruler of an independent Haiti.

How did we not know all of this?

The beauty of Haitian Creole, spoken by the island's locals, enthralled Alicen and me, and we were also transfixed by Haitians who spoke fluent French.

We even ventured into Port-au-Prince one day, despite the warnings from the local people to steer clear of the capital city. Kidnappings of women and children had surged over the years as gang violence worsened. Before we arrived, the country's president, Jovenel Moise, was assassinated. That only fueled widespread political instability.

The devastation we witnessed in the Capitol broke our hearts. Haiti is described as the poorest country in the Western Hemisphere. As much as I wanted to cling to the image of their people fighting for their freedom from the French and make that the prevalent narrative in my head, I could not deny what my eyes were seeing.

Rampant sickness, filthy streets, a lack of clean water and medical care, dilapidated homes, families sleeping in the street. Foreigners continued to devastate this country, and what makes it worse is the local government is allegedly complicit!

Greed, power, hubris, more important than humanity? Alicen and I were horrified.

I can't say that I've known many Haitians in my lifetime. I'm not sure if it's because they never told me they were from Haiti or because our paths literally did not cross. Sitting with the locals made me regret not knowing more about this history and how much it contributed to independence in America.

We headed back to Jacmel (racked with guilt). Alicen and I counted our blessings. We marveled that, despite all the pain and destruction, the people we spoke to were still loving, generous with their time and stories, and, surprisingly, full of smiles. Their indomitable spirit and triumphant resilience continue to radiate through battered bodies and toothless grins. Alicen and I vowed to never take our blessings for granted. We were so grateful for this glimpse into the soul of the downtrodden because it reminded us that no matter what you are going through, you can summon up a will to survive!

The country's breathtaking beauty seemed to mirror the radiance of the woman beside me, deepening our bond. We spent hours lounging on the beach, sipping Barbancourt, planning our future. I could not keep my hands off my beautiful wife. I also could not stop saying, *my beautiful wife.* Alicen would giggle each time I called her that. Her giddiness only made me say it more.

We made love, ate fresh fruit and seafood, napped, explored the island, and made love again...for five days. It never got old.

Caitlyn accurately described Jacmel as a haven for art, folklore, foodies, festivals, and nightlife. There was never a dull moment. Alicen and I fell deeply in love (again), and we agreed Haiti stoked our emotions.

I wished time could stretch indefinitely. However, the demands of our work schedules pulled us back to reality. The time came for us to bid farewell to our Haitian paradise and get home.

Curiously, throughout our honeymoon, Alicen hadn't mentioned her father. His conspicuous absence hung in the air like an unspoken question. Alicen's composure suggested her father's disappearing act did not discourage her. She had chosen her beloved Uncle Mike to walk her down the aisle.

Our plane touched down on U.S. soil, and a wave of anxiety came over me. We powered up our phones, and a deluge of notifications flooded the screen.

An unexpected call from Mr. Reynolds was among the flood of work-related messages. He had apparently grown concerned about his daughter (at least, that's what Alicen told me). I'm not sure why. I mean, did he think I was going to lock her in a basement after she said, "I do?"

The reasons behind his change of heart were never disclosed. Growing up with a father who exhibited similar traits, I understood the intricate dynamics at play within their relationship and respectfully gave them their space.

Meanwhile, I had questions of my own that needed answering. I looked forward to connecting with my mother and learning about the aunt I had never known existed.

According to my mother's tearful account, my grandfather had disowned my aunt after high school because she fell in love with another woman when she began college. This love defied societal norms and did not align with her father's close-minded thinking. My mother carried the burden of guilt. She acknowledged that her father's influence forced her to be complicit in the separation.

After my grandfather's passing, she contemplated reuniting with her beloved sister; however, she met with vehement opposition from my father. He adamantly declared that such a reunion would never happen within the walls of his supposed "Godly residence."

My father's hate mystified me. The fact my aunt was erased from our family narrative only fueled the question of how one could harbor such abhorrence towards their flesh and blood. In my grandfather's world, the tenet of "hate the sin, love the sinner" did not exist, undermining the very foundations of his Christian faith.

As I walked away from the suffocating confines of that household, I witnessed firsthand the dissonance between professed faith and unchristian-like behavior. People like my father and grandfather used their religious convictions as a shield, cloaking themselves in self-righteousness while disregarding the core message of the love and compassion Jesus preached. It was a painful realization, an awakening to the imperfections and contradictions that existed within the realm of faith.

I refused to let the darkness of hypocrisy overshadow the true foundation of Christianity. I held fast to the belief that there were genuine followers of Christ, those who embodied the principles of love, acceptance, and forgiveness. With hope in my heart, I intended to reconnect with my aunt and bridge the gap created by my family's narrow-mindedness.

It was also my time to get to know the remarkable woman who agreed to be my wife. If I ever doubted there was a God, her willingness to say "I do" cast that aside.

The chapters of our lives were intertwined in ways we had yet to comprehend.

GAME NIGHT

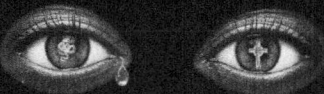

CHAPTER 11

"

Healing is a matter of time, but it is sometimes also a matter of opportunity.

HIPPOCRATES

As our journey unfolded, a sense of normalcy settled upon our lives. Everything started to come together at work, and at home.

Caitlyn, Alicen, and I became a trio of friends. We literally defied conventional friendship norms. Caitlyn and I, an unlikely pair, began to grow on each other in ways I hadn't anticipated. It was as if the universe made good on its infamous sense of humor and conspired to create this unlikely rapport.

To think it all started with a chance encounter in a classroom at the University of Kentucky and evolved into something I could only describe as a blessing. I'm not a particularly religious person, but I know a godsend when I feel one.

Alicen and I were comfortable in the groove of our everyday routine – basically, work, home, repeat. Our small apartment was cozy and had just enough furniture to make it relaxed, without being too crowded. I'm not sure if it was my military background or the fact that my father used to lose his shit at the slightest sign of clutter, but I was borderline OCD when it came to maintaining a neat environment. Alicen used to tease me, saying I was like the husband from **"Sleeping With the Enemy"** – minus the whole crazy, obsessed, homicidal husband thing, of course. She wasn't nearly as organized as me, and we butt heads sometimes about her unreasonable inability to shut off lights after leaving a room, or throwing food scraps directly into the trash instead of using the garbage disposal to avoid stinking up the place, but for the most part, she tried her best and to her credit was great at cleaning every inch of our 680 square foot residence from top to bottom. She always seemed pretty content with that, but when it came to laundry, not so much. It never failed, that the dirty clothes, towels, and sheets would pile right before the busiest week ever. We were either working extra hours, or I had to head out of town. Whatever the reason, she dreaded dragging those laundry bags down the six flights of stairs to the laundry room. God, forbid she forgets something after the first trip. Not good, for anyone! Still, Alicen never fell short when it came to being a homemaker and a caretaker. For that, I was always grateful. It helped me put the times we didn't get along in perspective. Once, during one of our impromptu talks at the kitchen table- you know the heavy discussions you didn't plan but appreciated having- she shared she felt the same about me.

That balance helped us get through challenges. If I could only get her to remember to turn off those lights!

We weren't big on hitting the town, but we needed to shake things up a bit. One evening, at Alicen's company Christmas party which was held in this swanky hotel nearby, we started talking to another couple. Alicen had mentioned the guy, Jason, a few times. He was the facilities manager and one of the only people she said she could talk to without nodding off! His wife Sophia worked at the Federal Reserve Bank in Chicago. The more we talked, we realized we found our couple twins.

They were an interracial couple, who met back in college, and they did the whole long-distance thing for a year before Jason moved to Chicago. Suddenly, our friend circle got an upgrade.

We'd begun having standing game nights, a bi-monthly ritual that became a high point of our busy lives. That's when I found out my wife was also an amazing host! She'd be up early prepping the food, and setting up the makeshift bar, and once the guests arrived, there was an endless flow of the best wings, quesadillas, ribs, sliders, you name it. She also served up specialty drinks everyone loved, and she did it all with a smile.

Those evenings were filled with laughter, conversations, and the release of pent-up stress. We played a different game each time (who knew there were so many board and card games!), and that added an element of surprise to our gatherings. It also kept our get-togethers from being predictable and boring.

The more we interacted with Jason and Sophia, the more I realized, I was pretty closed off at UK. I hadn't made many friends back then. Once Alicen and I got together, she became my world, my confidante. Because I was just getting out of the military, the age gap and differing interests made it hard to relate to fellow students. Sports had always been my go-to, but I didn't have any interest in any of the teams on campus, and doing anything without Alicen was not an option. These game nights helped me connect with like-minded individuals, step out of my comfort zone, and embrace the joy of friendship.

Believe it or not, Caitlyn and I partnered up a few times when we played spades, another sign we were getting past the initial **"why does this guy always have to monopolize my best friend's time"** period. Alicen didn't have a clue about playing spades. I was surprisingly good at it (a fact that gets a huge laugh from our black friends every time it comes up). **I picked up the finer points of spades while in the Navy.** Those spades tournaments on the mess decks became epic! I must admit, I definitely have some skills.

With Alicen's black card revoked, Caitlyn became the obvious choice. She was a dam good partner. We read each other as if we'd been playing for years, all eye contact, no talking across the table. We were so good at bidding, that everyone would think we must be cheating! She was just that good, and so was I.

One night we played a popular trivia game, and I started thinking, there's a **subtle racial bias** in some of these questions. They seemed to lean heavily towards topics and pop culture that were more relatable to a predominantly white audience. It's like the questions assumed a certain background knowledge that didn't align with the experiences of some of my black friends. Whether it was classic sitcoms, iconic movie quotes, or historical events, I felt like the topics were inadvertently excluding those who didn't share the same cultural references.

Jason, who was black, blew up my theory. He was particularly good at those games. Probably because he grew up watching different shows, listening to different music, and reading different books than I (and others we hung out with) did. He was intelligent and easygoing, far from what some might consider "corny." He reminded me of the actor Taye Diggs; clean-cut, ready for business, smart, but still chills at the barber shop with his boys, talking about sports. I knew all about Diggs because Alicen and Caitlyn watched the movie "The Best Man" over a hundred times (at least it seemed that way), giggling and fawning over all the main male characters.

As Jason knocked down question after question, it was clear; It wasn't about race, it was about the different backgrounds we came from and the varied activities that shaped our interests.

That didn't make losing easier though. Jason and Sophia wiped the floor with us!

One night, Caitlyn introduced the idea of ancestry DNA tests. She'd read about DNA reveal parties, and we decided to dedicate our next game night to exploring our genetic heritage. We all pitched in and purchased our testing kits (which were not cheap). We all prepped before taking our tests by brushing our teeth and making sure we didn't eat, or drink for the mandatory 30 minutes based on the instructions on the box. We all passed the time by making wild guesses about our ancestry. Of course, Caitlyn, who was always proud of her Haitian roots, stood confident in her predictions.

The rest of the night was spent eating, catching up on what's been going on in our lives, and enjoying each other's company. We made plans to reconvene in two months with our DNA results. We agreed it would be a cool idea if everyone prepared a dish representing our newly discovered cultural origins. I couldn't help but stake my claim on the griot and black rice dish Caitlyn had once prepared—a taste of her Haitian heritage.

After everyone left and Alicen fell asleep, I started to clean up. **When we moved in together, we agreed if she did the cooking, I would take care of the dishes and get the kitchen spotless.** I actually liked cleaning the kitchen. It was therapeutic for me. Not to mention, Alicen loved walking into a clean kitchen to prepare a hot cup of coffee in the morning. That was her thing, and I did my best to make sure I obliged.

When I was done, I sat in the living room, looking out the window and appreciating the stillness, the quiet. I was grateful for the life we were building together. Moments of joy, camaraderie, and shared laughter became a foundation for our relationship. It was more than just game nights; it was about creating memories, fostering a sense of belonging, and looking ahead to a promising future.

MAKE ME A PROMISE

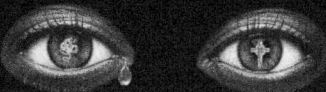

CHAPTER 12

"

By all means, marry. If you get a good wife, you'll become happy; if you get a bad one, you'll become a philosopher.

SOCRATES

M y five-year work anniversary approached, and I felt a sense of accomplishment. Life was going well.

I received frequent calls from Mom, sharing the happiness she and her sister had found in each other's company. It was heartwarming to hear them reminisce like they were kids again. I loved knowing that Mom had someone close to lean on and who could help with my brother.

My aunt was content being back in Kentucky. Times had changed, and a more progressive atmosphere prevailed. Though it wasn't quite like Chicago, Kentucky transformed in ways that surprised me.

Alicen understood the demanding nature of my grueling work hours, and I tried to reciprocate her support. She came home emotionally exhausted from her job at the Cook County facility. That was not the case when she was at the privately owned mental health facility where she cut her teeth. She despised the snobby attitude that came with working at a private hospital. Still, the county facility took its toll in other ways.

Days grew longer, nights became shorter, and I noticed a subtle change in the love that had once radiated between us. Discussions about having children got lost amid the stress of Alicen's job and my countless nights away from our bedroom.

"We will get through this," I reassured myself privately. "Just another hill to climb."

After one very tense Christmas, Alicen and her father made amends. Later in the Spring Mr. Reynolds and I resumed our tradition of guy time on the back nine. I looked forward to our outings.

"Here we are, young man. This is getting kind of old. Are you ever going to beat me?" Mr. Reynolds teased, displaying his impressive golfing skills.

"I can only hope, sir," I replied with a smile.

"We've been at this for almost ten years! Are you sure you're not just taking it easy on an old man?"

"No, Sir. I give it my all each time. You're just that good," I replied, trying to concentrate on the game despite his distractions.

"Martin, can I ask you something?" he said, catching me off guard.

I sensed tension. The last time those words were spoken between us didn't end well.

"Yes, sir," I replied cautiously.

"Are you and my baby girl ever going to give us a grandchild?" he asked, unwittingly bringing up a difficult topic.

I paused, trying to navigate the delicate situation.

"We definitely plan to, sir. We're both focused on building our careers right now."

He sighed.

"Women and careers... I'm still trying to get used to that, young man. In my day, wives kept the home. That was a full-time job.

He paused, longing for what he felt were the good old days, reflecting on his values and the changing times.

"I'm proud of my daughter, but I want the Reynolds lineage to continue."

"I understand," I replied.

"Well, I'm glad you understand because I'm counting on you," he said, his words trailing off, leaving me with a sense that there was more on his mind.

The day drew to a close. I couldn't shake the feeling that Mr. Reynolds hadn't said everything he wanted to. It was like he was grappling with something, his unspoken thoughts hanging in the air.

"How much do you like your job?" he suddenly asked, catching me off guard again.

"Huh?" I responded, taken aback by the unexpected question.

"Have you ever considered doing anything else?" he continued, delving into an unfamiliar line of inquiry.

I felt my discomfort growing. I had never been involved in any disagreements between Alicen and her dad. I tried my best not to get caught in the middle. Was this his way of trapping me in one of their feuds, trying to make me pick sides? I was not in the mood for this drama but remained engaged. And cautious.

"Well," I began, trying to maintain my composure.

"What did you have in mind, Mr. Reynolds?"

"A friend of mine seems to think you would be a perfect candidate to represent our district in Washington," he revealed. You remember David, the City Council member we talked to a while back?"

I was utterly baffled. I remember a brief encounter with that guy, but we never discussed politics, let alone anything that would suggest potential candidacy. How did Mr. Reynolds even know my political leanings?

"Sir, if you don't mind me asking, why does he think that?"

"I know you're a man of values. And in the brief exchange we all had, he agreed. People have a sense about these things, Marty. That alone says a lot about you in this generation," he replied, offering some insight.

"Not to mention, as I always say, life is not complicated, people are."

He was always so pleased with himself when he used that phrase.

"If you know, you know," he continued. "It doesn't take a whole lot of talking and interaction."

I couldn't argue with that. Maybe Alicen shared the book from our first project with him.

"Thank you, sir."

He nodded with satisfaction.

"But..."

His smile faded.

"If I were to consider it, I would need to discuss it with Alicen and hear her perspective," I said, realizing how much I valued her opinion. "When do I have to give him an answer?"

"Let's schedule our next back nine venture for next Saturday instead of waiting until next month. You can ask him all these questions since I don't have the answers," he proposed, leaving me both curious and anxious about what lay ahead.

When I got home, I was overjoyed to see Alicen's car parked in her assigned parking spot. Even after all these years, the thought of her still gave me butterflies. Whether it was the conversation with her father or simply missing her, I knew our evening would be lively. I was eager to share my talk with her that I had with her dad, confident she would see beyond the surface and provide me with valuable insights.

She was ending a phone call.

"Who was that?" I asked.

"Oh, just Dr. Herzik from work," she replied casually.

"Is everything alright?"

"Yeah, we were just discussing a new patient," she assured me.

"Okay, good."

Here goes.

"Baby, I need to ask you a very serious question. Please give it some deep thought before you respond."

"Oh boy," she muttered playfully. "Go ahead, shoot."

With a mix of eagerness and trepidation, I asked, "What do you think about me running for public office?"

"What? I did not know that was even on your radar. Did I miss something?" she exclaimed, surprised by the unexpected topic.

"Your dad approached me about it today," I explained. "Apparently, he sees me as a suitable candidate and us as the perfect couple."

I watched as Alicen processed the information, listening attentively. After a moment, she spoke, her voice a mix of reflection and resolve.

"I have one condition."

My eyes narrowed, unsure of what she was about to say.

"I want you to make real gun legislation a major focus. If you're willing to do that, I'm on board," she declared.

I was shocked. Politicians and the current President, whose controversial reign had caused division, frustrated Alicen. I would be running on the same ticket during his re-election campaign.

"I know that issue is close to your heart, babe. Of course, I can definitely do that."

"Look, Marty, we should stop relying on the "system" to protect our youth. We can't put their futures in the hands of lawmakers who don't give a damn about them. However, knowing that there would be someone on Capitol Hill who is as invested in this crisis as I am makes me feel better."

I weighed my next statement.

"Ali, laws of the land are not personal. They are passed for the collective..."

I could not finish my thought before she interrupted, and I could feel her energy shift from supportive wife to fierce anti-gun lobbyist in the blink of an eye.

"Yeah, and generally, they draft them to protect the interests of a select few."

Here we go.

"Newsflash, Marty, people that look like my brother are not always part of that chosen group."

I wanted her to be very clear about one thing (but feared an argument loomed). No matter how invested I was in the issue, I could not make any promises because that is not how our political process works.

Alicen, babe, no politician (as far as I know) sits down and says, "Let's customize *this legislation* for Mr. and Mrs. Reynolds. We want to make sure their son can walk in his family's neighborhood without fear of being gunned down based on his appearance."

She exhaled heavily, and I could tell she was ready to tear into me. The memory of losing her brother was driving an innate fury about to bubble to the surface.

I tried to change my tone without changing the subject.

"Ali, we talked about this, especially when you and I discussed having our own children back in the day.

She narrowed her eyes at the passive-aggressive dig but didn't challenge me.

"We both agreed we need to rely on *reality checks and balances*. It starts at home, remember?" I asked. "We have to teach our children that, not that long ago, people who looked like them weren't even considered a whole person. They were chattel. Expendable."

She relaxed, clearly assuaged by my sensitivity and understanding of history.

"I see you've been paying attention in class," she responded with too much snark for my taste, but I let that go.

"Well, I had an excellent teacher," I replied, trying to diffuse the tension. "One of the greatest lessons I learned is, because of the efforts of many and the resolve of others, African Americans could evolve past horror into nightmare, into fear, into caution, and hopefully, into varying degrees of hope because..."

She interrupted...

"But we still have to fight for the "dream," and we have yet to know acceptance. So, to shut them down, we must teach this new generation that they have to be successful, smart, run for office, get a degree."

"Looks like we just wrote my campaign speech," I said proudly.

She smiled. It had been a long time since we talked like this, and it felt like home.

My lovely wife, who always had to have the last word, interrupted the moment of bliss.

"All I'm saying is, sometimes we talk too much. We need to teach kids from underserved communities and privileged homes to become productive citizens people will listen to. We need to help shape these young minds in ways that inspire them to enact change, no matter how small."

She was pontificating, but I did not interject.

"They need to focus on becoming decision-makers instead of someone who allows decisions to be made for them."

I paused, unsure if she was done.

"Oh, and one more thing!" she added with emphasis. **"Promise me you won't make any appearances with the current President. I can't stand him."**

"That's a no-brainer," I replied with a smile. "Consider it done."

We discussed this potential critical shift in our lives and weighed the pros and cons of being in the public eye. Ultimately, we agreed people listen to those who can do something for them or *to* them. That is where the power is. We also agreed that should I decide to run, we were both committed to developing a political platform designed to make a difference.

Possibilities hung in the air.

With the prospect of a political career on the horizon, the path ahead seemed uncertain but exciting.

Little did I know the challenges and revelations that awaited us on the journey would change our lives forever.

DREAM SEQUENCE

"

The best way to resolve any problem in the human world is for all sides to sit down and talk.

Dalai Lama

The roaring sound of uncontrolled waves was deafening. At this moment, water, which had been everything from a source of life to an escape from my reality, was the enemy. How the hell did this happen?

"Shit, I'm trapped."

I panicked, realizing Alicen was not by my side.

"Alicen!" I yelled. "Ali, babe, answer me!"

I was confused.

How did we both end up on the Dubuque? Was I dreaming again? Another nightmare? I hadn't experienced night terrors in so long. I prayed this was a dream, but it felt so real!

"Alicen!"

She didn't respond.

"Ali, don't leave me, please!" I pleaded. "Answer me!"

I panicked. I tried walking toward the hatch, but the density of the rushing water limited my steps. I was on the verge of drowning in what should have been a secure and watertight chamber.

I heard someone else in the chamber with me as I struggled to find a way out. I whipped around to see a distorted figure a few feet away, the face unidentifiable in the dark, damp chamber.

"Ali, babe, is that you? Are you ok?"

The shape was too big to be my wife, yet somehow, I felt like I knew this person. I did not recall ever crossing paths with a man of that build, at least not on the ship, but then again, it was a big ass ship.

I tried to get his attention. Whoever the hell he was, I needed him to help me get to Alicen.

"What's the plan, man? We need to get out of here!"

Silence.

"Hey, I'm fucking talking to you, bro. It's Ruane."

Crickets.

"Do I know you? Because we need to figure this out. I can't die here!"

Nothing.

I realized I was getting nowhere with this freak. Maybe the guy was scared, but this was not the time to be a punk.

Words and thoughts had become muddled, fraught with tension, dread.

"Hey! Look at me, asshole!" I shouted. "Why won't you look at me?"

The water continued to rise. I knew time was running out. I thought about Alicen, my mom, my brother.

Damn, I was just talking to Mr. Reynolds. Life was getting better.

These must be the come-to-Jesus conversations you have with yourself when you contemplate your mortality and fear the end is near.

Searching for an outlet for my apprehension, I began blaming the unknown figure for our current predicament. This guy was useless, selfish, and heartless. Who just lets people suffer? What kind of evil informs this inaction in the face of tragedy? I wondered why I had to be trapped with this individual.

I was getting more and more agitated.

"Jesus, not like this. This can't be how it ends," I whispered to myself.

"I didn't live life to the fullest."

The awareness burned my soul.

I wish I could go back and do more. Be a better husband, son, and brother.

As the rippling waves passed my waist, I looked around the chamber, recalling every detail of the complex make-up of the ship. I cursed the multi-million-dollar construction of the vessel, wondering why it had failed me at this critical moment.

I wondered how much longer it would be before I was completely submerged?

My mute, mysterious shipmate loomed even more ominously and still refused to utter a word. I felt an eerie familiarity wash over me as I struggled to make out this guy's features.

Suddenly, he turned toward me, eyes flashing and an odd smile forming below a large bulbous nose. I stared in horror. I spoke, no, stammered, the words burning the back of my throat.

I spit out the only phrase I could manage...

"How the hell did you get here?"

A DEAL WITH THE DEVIL

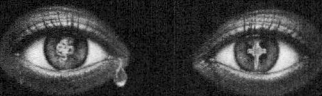

CHAPTER 13

"

If a man repeats a lie over and over, he will eventually accept the lie as truth. Moreover, he will believe it to be the truth.

NAPOLEON HILL

I shot straight up, sweat pouring down my body. I immediately reached for Alicen to make sure she was beside me. She was. Thank God. I let out a sigh of relief and cuddled up next to her, getting as close as I could without pushing her off the bed. I usually have bad dreams ahead of big events taking place in my life, but this last nightmare really shook me up. I don't believe in "interpreting" dreams. However, there was some hidden meaning in this one.

I pressed my face into Alicen's neck. Her scent relaxed me, and I was able to fall asleep.

Still, the disturbing effects of the dream lingered.

The next Guy Time on the Back Nine gathering was quite a celebration. I still couldn't quite understand why they were so interested in me, but I was willing to give it a shot. I knew the important topics of discussion: tax cuts, smaller government, and, of course, the pro-life versus pro-choice debate. The current President had mentioned concerns about free speech and the push for a wall on the Southern border, but those weren't my top priorities. I needed to find a way to introduce Alicen's vision of a new America, which included gun control.

At my first town hall meeting, there were around thirty people in attendance.

I stepped into the local public-school gymnasium. The fluorescent bulbs buzzed overhead, casting a sterile, slightly harsh glow on the room. It wasn't exactly the warm ambiance I had pictured, but it seemed fitting for the serious tone of the evening.

The chairs were arranged in neat rows, facing a small stage at the front of the room. I noticed how close they were to one another. As someone who values personal space and respects the fact that others may feel the same way, I was not impressed by this part of the planning.

Two microphones stood on stands at the center of the stage for the candidates. I glanced at them nervously, knowing they would soon carry my voice across the room. I had practiced my talking points countless times, but knowing I was about to be standing in front of a crowd and delivering my ideas was intimidating.

Reporters from various local news outlets were scattered throughout the audience, their cameras, and notepads ready to capture moments that would define this town hall meeting. Their presence reminded me that the local community and beyond would dissect and analyze my words and actions. I knew I had probably bitten off more than I could chew. Still, I had to push through, not just for myself but for the expectations of my father-in-law, wife, and, most importantly, myself. **Failure was not an option.**

As the crowd settled and the meeting began, **I hoped my words would resonate, and I did not disappoint those who believed in me.** After a long introduction from the moderator, he turned the floor over to the attendees.

"Here we go," I whispered to myself.

The first question came from a middle-aged man who seemed well-off. He asked the typical question, **"Where do you stand on taxes, young man?"** It seemed like he felt overtaxed, so I tried to give an answer that would please him. **"There are too many,"** I replied. **"If elected, I'll do my best to reduce taxes on the middle class."**

He nodded and started writing. That was the end of his questions for me that night. Some others touched on the same topic, but that passed quickly.

I thought, if this is how it's going to be, **I think I can handle this!**

The next 15 minutes were spent fielding questions about enhancing community safety, addressing deteriorating road infrastructure, and considering a shorter school year.

I was on a roll. This was not too bad.

Eventually, we reached the pressing subject of abortion. The night wouldn't be complete without knowing my stance on pro-life versus pro-choice.

"I'm not sure when this became such a divisive discussion," I began.

"I've never met anyone openly discussing terminating a pregnancy. From what I know, I only see one way—pro-life." I continued, "**I want to share that I have a younger brother who is mentally challenged, and I couldn't imagine my life without him. That's why I can't fathom any reason to end a life. I want to be a strong voice that makes that clear to everyone.**"

That statement caught the attention of everyone in the room.

"Any more questions?" I asked, but the room fell silent. "If not, I want all of you to get home safely. It's been a pleasure spending this evening with you."

As the crowd left the room, it felt like the handshakes would go on forever. Fortunately, they were accompanied by declarations of support. I couldn't wait to share the experience with Alicen.

Back home, she wasted no time in questioning me about the event.

"How did it go?" she asked, excitement evident in her voice.

"It was awesome, babe. I wish you could have been there. I wrapped my arms around her in a hug.

"Well," she prompted, "did they like you?"

"I think so," I replied. "I hope so. At least, it seemed that way."

The smile on her face never faded. "How did they react to your stance on guns?"

"You know what? No one even asked me about that."

"So... you made sure to bring it up, right?"

"It doesn't quite work that way, babe. They ask the questions, and I provide the answers," I explained.

She gave me "the look." The sideways glance that meant she wanted to go off but was restraining herself.

"You're still committed to the promise you made, right?"

"Of course, sweetheart. Your opinion means more to me than anyone else's. Even if it means not winning, our marriage comes first."

"Marty, don't blow sunshine up my ass. I knew this would happen!"

It will never cease to amaze me how this woman can go from zero to a hot 10 on the mood meter in a matter of seconds.

"Ali, I can't just walk into a town hall meeting and start making public statements off the dome. There is a process, babe."

"Seriously, Marty, fuck the 'process.' When we talked about you running, the 'process' is one of the things we both agreed was messed up. And now, here you are spewing the party line rhetoric!"

"Are you serious right now, Alicen?"

"As a heart attack."

It took all I had not to shake her until her eyes rolled into the back of her head.

"Ok, Alicen, tell me what I was supposed to do."

The look in her eyes and the way her head cocked to one side let me know she was about to go nuclear.

"You were supposed to have the balls to tell them that gun legislation in this country is non-existent, and people are dying because the NRA would rather trade profit for lives. You do still have them, right?"

"Have what?"

"Your balls, Marty, or have you put them on the chopping block to cinch your position on the campaign trail."

I'd had enough.

"Alicen, you need to back off. Now! Your beef is with the bastardization of the Second Amendment, not me. I didn't write the legislation! And for your information, a hell of a lot more people believe the right to keep and bear arms shall -quote- not be infringed. I am not about to go in guns blazing, challenging an already heated issue."

She glared at me.

"And yes, pun intended," I said with an attitude.

She doubled down.

"**You are a hypocrite, Martin.** You talk a good game about rights, principles, and values. You have people thinking you are this noble, thoughtful, genuine guy. Meantime, you are lying. Lying to them, to me, and definitely to yourself."

My head was spinning.

"You are acting like a lunatic, Alicen."

"Whatever Martin. I practically handed you a script. You didn't even have to think about what to say. We had an entire conversation about this! I even proposed a solution."

"Alicen, it was a suggestion, not a solution."

"Oh, because *you* didn't come up with it, it's just a suggestion? Got it."

She was off the rails.

"**Alicen, it's a good idea.** I've thought long and hard about it. Proposing that **guns need to be registered** when purchased like all vehicles operating on public roads and highways is genius."

I figured **praising the idea might calm her down.**

"Exactly!" she bellowed. "**Because it will begin a paper trail that originates with the purchaser.** The owner would also have to bring in the firearm annually to undergo checks and balances that confirm it is still in the hands of the original owner."

"I just said it was a great idea, Alicen. You don't have to go through the entire spiel. Again." She was off the rails.

She rolled her eyes.

"Like I told you when we first talked about this, I definitely like the part about charging a fee for the process, making sure some of the payments are allocated to foundations or certified medical facilities dedicated to studying and treating mental illness."

"So, you *were* listening," she said.

"I told you I was. But you are so busy projecting your anger about *whatever* you got going on in your life, you can't see past your feelings."

"Projecting? Dude, that is so offensive!" she scoffed.

"Oh, and nothing you've said is offensive?" I snapped. "Unbelievable."

"You know what, Martin, I don't need this from you."

She stomped into our bedroom, snatched pillows and the comforter from the bed, and retreated to the guest bedroom.

We had promised to never go to bed angry. We swore that we would always stop and think about how devastating that could be to our marriage. Nothing should ever rise to the level of sleeping in separate beds.

That night, promises were broken, and a chasm formed in our relationship.

Fortunately, I was able to put my personal issues aside and carry on with my campaign.

My approach struck a chord with the 50-plus age group, who appreciated my straightforwardness and values. It was a demographic that understood the importance of tradition and conservative ideals.

As a new candidate who wasn't a career politician, stepping onto the campaign trail was a whirlwind experience. I didn't have the polished rhetoric or the political maneuvering skills seasoned politicians possessed. Instead, I relied on my authenticity and spoke from the perspective of my principles.

The growing support I received from college students caught me off guard.

I was far from being the popular guy on campus in college. I hadn't undergone a drastic transformation since then, so it was astonishing to see young individuals responding positively to my message. Maybe they were tired of the political status quo and sought a genuine voice that could relate to their concerns.

Navigating the campaign trail as a non-politician had its challenges. I lacked the insider knowledge and connections that career politicians enjoyed. Every step forward a learning experience. I did my best to understand the intricacies of fundraising, grassroots organizing, and public speaking.

It was a constant balancing act; trying to stay true to my principles while appealing to diverse voters.

Yet, despite the challenges, momentum was building. Somehow, I had become a favorite among people nationwide who were yearning for a fresh perspective. The support and enthusiasm I witnessed at events and rallies were sometimes overwhelming. It was as if my candidacy had ignited a sense of hope and possibility. I was humbled and grateful for the opportunity to make a difference, even if I wasn't your typical politician.

Regardless of the audience, my talking points remained consistent.

The President was on the campaign trail, and I avoided him. With my newfound popularity and his need to appeal to younger voters, I knew it was only a matter of time before the National Committee approached me about appearing with him. With that in mind, I focused on making gun control a central topic in all my interviews. The current President had heavy backing from the NRA during his political campaigns. The agency spent around $30 million to support his Presidential bid, making it the largest amount the organization had ever spent on a candidate. They often cited his commitment to protecting Second Amendment rights to validate their support.

I was convinced there was no way he would risk having me share a stage with him at a rally.

UNIMAGINABLE TRAUMA

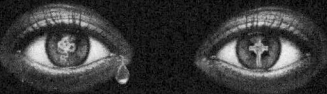

CHAPTER 14

"

True love cannot
be found where it
does not exist, nor
can it be denied
where it does.

TORQUATO TASSO

The days following our volcanic blow-up were confusing, to say the least. Part of me was so mad at Alicen for attacking me the way she did, pelting me with baseless accusations, trying to hurt me with her words. How can someone be so mean to a person they claim to love?

On the other hand, I grappled with my vows, the promises we made in front of the Pastor, and in the privacy of our intimate moments. I took all that seriously. Still, when is enough, enough? Some lines should not be crossed.

I seriously could not rationally reconcile my argument with Alicen in my head! I have to say, it was probably the most unreasonable and contentious disagreement we've had. The fact that neither of us has spoken more than two words to one another tells me she has not budged on her stance.

That stubborn, petulant behavior stopped being adorable a long time ago.

Months ago, I would have given in. Maybe I was blinded by love. Or I was so accustomed to being on the defensive most of my life that I'd wave the white flag at the first sign of hostility to keep the peace. Since Alicen and I met (literally, that first day in Psychology class), I've done everything I can to be the voice of reason in our relationship. I've known she can be quite…passionate about her beliefs. This time, however, I cannot cede to her irrational outburst.

The night of our disagreement, I lay in bed thinking, I am sick and tired of always being the bigger person. I will shed some of that weight from now on and shrink down to her level of petty.

But then again, is it really petty if you know you have done nothing wrong?

Whenever I took a break from the campaign trail and spent time at home, Alicen and I didn't say much to each other. There were moments when, admittedly, I felt lost. Who do you turn to when your best friend becomes your worst enemy? I wondered if this stalemate was even worth it. You get so many days in a lifetime; why spend any of them mad at your spouse?

Then we'd pass each other in the hallway, and I could feel the animosity seep out of her pores and think, nah, I'm good.

This went on for a few days. I'd come home, and Alicen would leave. She and Caitlyn were going out more, to where I'm not sure. Alicen was becoming more aloof and dismissive. I matched her mood for mood. The strain of campaigning was exhaustive enough. Dealing with unnecessary drama was not an option. Ironically, I made my case for gun control at a local meet and greet one evening. I shared some ideas Alicen had developed with voters. They loved them! I started to hurry home to share the experience with her. Then I remembered she probably wasn't there.

"I'm over this," I mumbled under my breath, dreading walking into the toxic atmosphere that had become our home.

Moments after expressing my angst about being around Alicen, she called. When I saw her name appear on the dashboard, I felt a flash of relief and then happiness. That didn't last long. I reminded myself that she has not been the kindest person these days. I wouldn't be surprised if she called because she needed me to do something for her or just wanted to argue again.

I hit ignore and turned up my favorite Sirius XM channel. **Nothing like some old-school hip-hop to fuel your "I don't give a dam" vibes.**

Seconds later, another call. She's nothing if not persistent.

Ignore.

One minute later, another call. I wondered if I should answer.

I turned down the music and called Alicen back. Straight to voicemail. What kind of game is this woman playing? I was not in the mood for this childish nonsense.

I was dialing her number again when I got another call, this time from a private number. I rarely answer when I don't know who is on the other end, but something told me I needed to pick up.

"Hello?"

"Martin, this is Dr. Herzik. I work with your wife at the clinic."

Did this woman have someone else call me because I ignored her call?

"How can I help you?"

He paused, sighed, and said, "It's about Alicen."

I felt my heart drop.

"What about her? What's going on? Is she there? Let me talk to her?" I rambled.

"Martin, please try to remain—"

"Where the hell is my wife?" I yelled.

"Please come to the clinic as soon as possible," he asked calmly.

"Is she..." I could not get the words out.

"Alicen is okay, but she really needs you to come now."

I don't know how many traffic laws I broke racing to the clinic, but I didn't care. All I could think was that I should never have stopped talking to her. The guilt rushed over me, and I knew I would never forgive myself if the last moments of our lives together had been spent in a stalemate, a senseless battle to prove who could hold out longer with the silent treatment.

I prayed.

"God, please let her be okay, and I promise I will never let anything make me this angry again. Please don't take her from me. Please."

As I walked in, Alicen sat in her office looking like she'd been in a fight. Her scrubs were torn at the neck, and there were scratches on both her arms. She had obviously been crying, judging by her bloodshot eyes. I started toward her.

"Ali, baby, what happened? Who hurt you?"

When I ran to her, two police officers stopped me.

"I'm trying to talk to my wife. What are you doing?"

"Sir, we are still questioning her?"

I was dumbfounded.

"Questioning her? About what? What's going on?" I snarled.

"Sir, I'm going to have to ask you to either remain calm or step outside."

Ali looked up at me with tears in her eyes. I needed answers, but she needed me to settle down and not make things worse. I took a deep breath, forced a weak smile, mouthed, "I love you, baby," and walked outside with Dr. Herzik.

"Alicen was overpowered by a male patient today," he said.

I flinched, resisting the urge to break down the door and strong-arm my way past the police to my wife.

"Overpower...what does that mean?" I asked.

"She was sexually assaulted."

"What! You mean raped? Somebody raped my wife?"

My legs felt like they were buckling.

He placed his hand on my shoulder and made eye contact.

"Do you need to sit down?"

I probably should have, but my legs wouldn't move.

"No, I just want to be with Alicen."

"Yes, of course. I'm not sure of the details, Martin, but I know she's traumatized."

"Where is the animal that violated my wife?"

He blinked rapidly at my comment but seemed to understand my frustration.

"He's being detained and examined by our doctors."

I lost it.

"Detained? This piece of crap raped my wife, and you are giving him an annual physical? Why the hell isn't he in handcuffs?"

"We are doing everything we can to make sure the situation is handled appropriately. There is a process."

There was that damn word again. Maybe Alicen was right. All these *processes* were more of a hindrance than a solution!

I stood in the waiting room for what seemed like hours. When they finally led her to me, she was unrecognizable. I had never seen her so shaken up, so fragile and vulnerable. I wanted to lay hands on the savage that did this to her. And by lay hands, I mean drill him in the chest with a full clip.

The irony was not lost on me.

Alicen fell into my arms, and we walked slowly out of the clinic and to my car. I didn't press her for any details on the ride home. I let her settle in, shower, and change into comfortable clothes before I carried her from the living room to the bedroom.

She slept for about an hour. I never left her side. I kept replaying images of how it probably transpired, picturing this animal forcing himself inside her and "hearing" her call out for me, and I was not there to protect her.

I felt my soul cave in.

Later that night, we sat on the couch, and Ali walked me through it. It was worse than I even imagined. The guy's mental illness meant he had no regard for how much he hurt her. He was not capable of forming that kind of empathy. If they had not pulled him off her in time, he would have killed her.

I felt angry, sad, and confused. I didn't even know something like this could happen there.

"I have to take an HIV test tomorrow," she said.

I didn't know how to react, so I simply said, "It'll be okay, baby. I'm here. I will never leave your side, no matter what."

"Martin," I heard the tremble in her voice. "I feel so dirty. You are the only man I have ever been intimate with. I never even considered being with anyone else."

That night, she cried herself to sleep.

DATE NIGHT

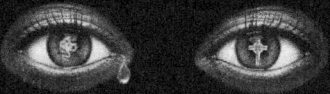

CHAPTER 15

"

I imagine one of the reasons people cling to their hates so stubbornly is because they sense, once hate is gone, they will be forced to deal with pain.

JAMES BALDWIN

My campaign gained momentum. The success was exhilarating. Beneath the surface, though, I felt anxious about my marriage. I adored Alicen. She was still the love of my life. But each day, it felt like our love was fading.

We didn't talk much about the rape. Every time I tried to bring it up or encourage her to work through it so she could start healing, she shut down. It's as if she thought ignoring the incident meant it never happened. No one ever knows how they will behave after surviving a tragedy. When you are in a relationship, the recovery process could bring you closer together or drive a wedge between you.

Alicen and I were drifting further apart.

She and Caitlyn continued to go out all the time. They spent more time together in the last few months than they did the entire time they were in college. Breakfast, brunch, dinner, drinks, coffee. It was always something.

My mind often wandered to my mom. Now, *that* relationship was consistent. She was the epitome of love in my life. If I had one wish, it would be that she lived long enough to find joy and make up for the years wasted being married to my father.

Days passed swiftly, and the campaign consumed me, becoming my refuge. Alicen, however, remained absent from this world. It seems ironic that the father she admired more than anything was the one who introduced me to this life, and she could care less about the whole prospect of my being elected.

Then it dawned on me.

The rape had deadened her emotions. It took her to a dark place. We had already been struggling. The dreaded "seven-year itch" (if such a thing existed) had reared its head. She started prioritizing her career and hanging out over our relationship. I spent more time talking to the press than my wife.

I thought about what my mom would say. Her words echoed in my mind,

"This, too, shall pass," she used to tell me. Especially when I was spinning out.

I prayed for her wisdom to wash over me.

Amid this tumultuous period, we talked about a date night during my last weekend at home before a weekslong campaign trip. I was surprised Alicen was receptive to the idea. We used to schedule special nights a lot when we dated and in the first couple of years of our marriage.

We agreed to work on *us* when I returned from the campaign trail.

One morning, as I waited for an Uber to take me to the airport, Alicen stepped out of the shower, her voice filled with a tenderness I hadn't heard in weeks.

"Babe," she whispered, her words laced with vulnerability. "I love you so much. Please, don't ever think any differently."

The weight of her love bore down upon me, a reminder of the depth of a connection beneath the surface.

"I love you too, Ali," I responded.

We kissed. It lacked the depth our desire once had, but remnants of the passion lingered.

"Now, I don't want to go," I confessed.

We shared a moment of laughter, a brief respite from the heaviness.

"Go out there and make the world a better place," she encouraged. Her words carried the enthusiasm I had been missing.

"We got this, Mrs. Ruane. Let no man put asunder."

"Amen, babe," she replied. "Amen."

"Now, let's change the world," we proclaimed in unison.

I hit the ground running.

From the bustling streets of Pennsylvania to the industrial landscape of Michigan, the vibrant energy of Florida, and the vast expanse of Texas, I traversed the campaign trail, tirelessly sharing my message, determined to make a positive impact on the world. Now, the Carolinas awaited. This was the heart of the Bible Belt, where the influence of the NRA and the strong pro-life sentiment loomed large.

My campaign manager warned me of the challenges that lie ahead. "This is where you change your talking points, Mr. Ruane," he advised, his voice filled with caution and urgency. I understood what he meant. In these communities, the stakes were high, and every word I uttered would be scrutinized by the media—FOX, CNN, MSNBC—waiting to pounce on any misstep.

The days blurred together. Fatigue settled in my bones. The constant travel, navigating through different time zones and climates, took its toll on my body and mind.

I underestimated the mental strain of this grueling journey.

"Eighteen stops in fourteen days," my manager emphasized, his tone conveying both weariness and determination. "You will probably lose track of where you are, but stay focused, Marty."

The guy was a mix of drill sergeant, motivational speaker, pastor, and pain in the ass. But he earned that paycheck.

"Remember to assert your pro-life stance and highlight your support for gun ownership," he stressed. "That's how you'll navigate these waters."

The words made me cringe. Alicen and I were finally in a good place. If she knew I had shifted the narrative on gun control, her head would explode...and so would our marriage.

The weight of guilt made me question if I could remain true to my principles amidst the intense pressure.

Next on the itinerary: Wisconsin. This was another battleground state where every word I spoke would be picked apart. One day, when my spirits were particularly low, my manager found a ray of sunshine in this volatile political tempest.

A flicker of weariness must have betrayed me as my manager's words took on an encouraging edge.

"Suck it up, Ruane," he blared. "This is the last stop before you go home to that beautiful wife of yours. Push through, give it your all, and then take time to rejuvenate."

He was right! It would be just five days before I would hold Alicen. He might as well have pumped caffeine straight into my veins!

As I prepared for the final leg of this demanding journey, I was running on pure adrenaline. I was also resolved to stay true to my convictions. The complexities of state laws and the deeply ingrained beliefs of the communities I would encounter were all part of the fight to create change.

When the final speech was delivered, the last debate in the books, and what seemed to be the millionth handshake, I was ready to see my wife.

I wanted to surprise Alicen. I would be home 2 days early and knew she would be excited. On the way, I stopped at her office with a dozen roses in hand.

Her face lit up as I approached.

"What are you doing here, wit yo sexy self?"

I grinned from ear to ear.

"I told them I quit!"

She pulled me closer and kissed me. "Yeah, right! Hey, are these for me?"

"Nah," I teased, "they're for my wife. You better make sure she gets them. She'll kill both of us!"

We laughed as she pulled the roses from my hand and sniffed each one.

"How long are you home?"

"Well, it looks like five days for now, but I don't want to speak too soon."

"Awesome," she replied.

We kissed again.

"I'll see you when you get home, babe. Don't work too hard," I said. "I love you."

As the days passed, I found myself thinking about how good things used to be between us.

Man, those early days with Alicen were something else. I can't help but smile when I think about our college days, especially our movie nights. We'd cram onto that beat-up couch, stuffing our faces with junk food and watching corny chick flicks or the latest Michael Bay and Jerry Bruckheimer action movie. And those study sessions? They always turned into movie marathons. But you know what was the best part? The talks we'd have in between, getting to know each other better with every cheesy line and laugh. It was a time when the relationship was new, untainted, and me and Alicen just loved being around each other.

Then there were our game nights with friends. The energy was always electric, and it felt like a mini reunion every time. We'd play board games for hours, laughing until our sides hurt, and there was this sense of genuine camaraderie that I really miss. But somewhere along the line, life got crazy. We got so caught up in everything that we forgot how to just enjoy each other's company.

Looking back, I realize I dropped the ball. I'm sorry for letting things get so tough between us. It's not just about trying anymore;

it's about stepping up and making this relationship work. I know it's a two-way street, but I also know I should take responsibility for my part. I'm committed to doing better, to appreciating every moment with Alicen, and showing her the love and respect she deserves.

Our date night was finally here. I was grateful another argument or some random work issues didn't get in our way.

Alicen was in the kitchen making her famous chicken quesadillas. It was my favorite dish, and it meant a lot that she chose to prepare it for our date. I was filling the silver beer bucket we had received as a wedding gift with ice. As I loaded it with beer, I ran my hand across the engraved rim. It read, *The Ruanes*.

"Yes, we are. Now and forever," I whispered.

We made our way to the couch. Before we sat down, I kissed her on her forehead, and she laid her hand gently on my chest.

It was going to be a good night.

As if on cue, the phone rang, shattering the promise of a loving moment.

My aunt's voice was urgent, foreboding. My heart sank.

Alicen lowered her head as she heard the conversation unfold. She could tell by my responses that our plans were on the verge of changing. Her expression was a mixture of concern and disappointment. I could feel her entire mood shift.

"I'm sorry, baby," I mouthed, trying to temper her discontent.

She was really looking forward to this movie. Denzel Washington was her favorite actor. She would often joke that he was the only man she would leave me for. I would quip back, "Shit, I'd let you!"

When I hung up, she said tentatively, "I recognized the voice on the other end. Your Aunt. What did she say?"

I fought back tears. The tone of my aunt's voice let me know something was wrong. Very wrong.

"She said I need to get home as soon as possible. It's my mom, but she wouldn't tell me what was going on with her."

"Well, that doesn't sound good," she said.

"No, no it doesn't. I just hope she's being dramatic."

"Me too. I'm sure it's fine, Marty. Think positively."

I welcomed the compassion my wife was showing. It had been a while since I'd felt that kind of understanding.

"Thanks, babe, I will. You coming with me?"

"Nah, I have some work to catch up on, and Caitlyn will be in town tomorrow, so I want to clear my assignments."

Her decision to prioritize her work and spend time with Caitlyn stung.

"Oh, okay. Well, guess that's that."

Yeah, you know how it is. She needs one of our *sisterventions* because something serious is happening in her life.

I was seething. Seriously? What could be more important than an emergency call about your mother-in-law? I resisted the urge to lash out.

Through clenched teeth, I responded, "Alright, I'll keep you posted."

It was too late to book a flight at this point, so I opted for the 5-and-a-half-hour drive instead. The time on the road would allow me to make some calls in case the campaign needed to be paused.

I arrived at my childhood home around 9 p.m. All the lights in my mom's house were out except for the one in her bedroom. I made my way down the hallway, my eyes struggling to adjust to the darkness. There was something heavy in the air, but I couldn't quite put my finger on it. I heard whispers and...crying?

I turned the corner, past the guest bathroom, to find my aunt, brother, and a priest at my mother's bedside.

When they moved away from the bed, my blood ran cold. My mother looked nothing like the woman I had known! Her face was so pale it seemed transparent. She was painfully thin and frail. Her nightgown hung loosely around her weakened frame, and her eyes looked right past me as if she were in a trance.

"What the hell is going on? Mom, what's wrong? You've been sick? Why didn't you tell me?"

Everyone hung their heads, averting their eyes, avoiding my questions. My brother just stared at my mom as she lay there, too weak to even sit up.

"Lance, are you okay? What is going on? Why won't anyone tell me what is going on?

Silence.
"Lance, look at me!"

He fell to his knees and grabbed my mom's hand. Her fingers appeared to melt into his palm. Her skin was so loose and gaunt.

Finally, my aunt managed to speak. Her words pierced through the room, crushing my spirit.

"The doctors say there is nothing more they can do."

My blood ran cold as the weight of those words settled upon me.

"Do? Do about what?" Jesus, Mom, what is happening?"

My mother looked at me, her eyes vacant. The room started spinning. I stood there, my heart pounding.

My aunt interrupted my daze.

"She was diagnosed with stage four pancreatic cancer four months ago, Marty."

I wanted to throw up.

"The doctors tried everything, very aggressive treatments for weeks, but the cancer kept spreading. It metastasized to her lungs and liver."

"No one told me..." I said, almost whimpering.

"Marty," my aunt's voice trembled with emotion, "she made us promise not to tell you. You know how your mom is. She didn't want you to get distracted or worry too much. She was so proud of everything you had going on and didn't want to be the reason you had to stop."

A tumultuous mix of emotions coursed through me. Disbelief, anger, and profound sadness flooded my soul. How could I not have known? How had I been oblivious to my own mother's battle with cancer?

The guilt washed over me. I had been too consumed by my own life, blinded by the success of a fucking political campaign, while my mother was dying.

My aunt led my brother out of the room, and the priest followed closely behind them. He turned to look at me before closing the door. I could tell he wanted to say something, anything, to give me strength. Words failed him. In a way, I was happy. Trite platitudes would only make the situation worse.

The door closed softly. I was alone with my mother.

I pulled a chair over to the bed and sat close, my face nearly touching hers.

Smiling, she whispered, "Son, I love you."

Tears welled up in my eyes as I held her hand tightly, responding, "I love you too, Mom."

She apologized, her voice trembling with the weight of her secret.

"I'm sorry for keeping this from you. I didn't want to burden or distract you from your path."

Her fragile voice wavered, desperate to convey her love and remorse.

"Marty, always remember one thing: I will always, always be watching over you and my beautiful Alicen. I am with you as you move through the twists and turns of life and marriage. That woman loves you, Marty. And you love her. Let that always be your 'why.'""

I sobbed uncontrollably.

"Yes, momma, I know you will always be with us."

In a feeble attempt at humor, she managed a gentle jab.

"When you become President one day, don't be like the jerk in office."

A faint smile tugged at the corners of her lips.

The room fell into a solemn silence. Her gaze met mine.

"I am so proud of the man you have become. Everything I sacrificed was worth it when I look at everything you have accomplished."

My heart ached. I have never known this kind of agony.

"Marty, I try not to ask too much of you."

"What is it, Mom? Anything you want,"

"Remember your promise to me. Please take care of your brother. Don't send him to a mental home. My soul would never rest?"

I didn't think twice.

"Yes, Mom, I remember. Lance will live with Alicen and me."

The moment hung in the air, heavy with emotions too intense to fully comprehend. A lump formed in my throat, and with tears streaming down my cheeks, I whispered, "I love you, Momma." It was a simple declaration, yet it carried the weight of a lifetime of gratitude and affection.

Then, as the final moments arrived, an indescribable despair washed over me. My mother's hand slipped from mine, her touch growing colder with each passing second. The realization of her absence enveloped me, and an overwhelming sense of loneliness settled deep in my soul.

I sat there for a minute, an hour, I don't even know.

I left to find my aunt. Her eyes, filled with sorrow, confirmed she knew what my heart couldn't bear to accept. My mother was gone.

Sobbing uncontrollably, I sought solace in my childhood bedroom, clinging to memories and fleeting glimpses of the past.

Alicen had been my constant companion since the day we met. For years, we never let a day pass without exchanging a goodnight and good morning. At that moment, I craved the comfort of her presence.

I called her... and called her... and called her. Each attempt went unanswered, and I resorted to texting her to make sure she couldn't blame me for not reaching out.

I didn't have time to dwell on her absence. Funeral arrangements had to be made, and I had to explain to my brother that Mom was with Dad. I also had to tell him he would be moving to Illinois.

On top of that, I had to locate the deed to the house, insurance policies, and all the responsibilities that accompanied burying a parent. I felt lost, unsure of where to even begin. When my father passed away, Mom took charge. Now, it was all on me.

The realization of how much I would miss her hit hard. I hadn't fully comprehended how much I relied on her for emotional support until that moment. I sought her advice on my marriage and marveled at her ability to calm my brother. We spoke every day.

Around 5:15 a.m., Alicen called, wide awake, driving to... somewhere. I mustered the strength to break the news. Her anguish echoed through the phone. Her bond with her parents ran deep, and the mere thought of losing them devastated her. This was as close as she had ever come to such a loss, and it tore at her heart. My mother's passing affected her deeply.

Overwhelmed by emotions, Alicen pulled the car over. She asked about the funeral and whether I had spoken to my brother.

"Speaking of him," I began, my voice quivering, "Mom asked me to promise that I would always take care of him and never put him in a mental home or hospital."

Pausing briefly, I continued, "She wants...wanted him to live with us, Alicen."

Silence.

The tension between us exploded.

"Are you there?" I asked.

"Yes," she finally replied, her voice weighed down.

I tried to change the subject.

"Where are—"

"To get Caitlyn," she interjected before I could finish. "She's at a hotel in the city, and she's very upset."

"Okay," I replied, my voice laden with weariness. "Well... keep me posted."

As the day wore on, I received a text from Alicen that read, **URGENT. CALL ASAP!!!!"**

I almost ignored her. Then I remembered the promise I made to God the night I thought I had lost her.

Still, I waited a bit before returning her call, bracing myself for what lay ahead.

THE MEMORIAL

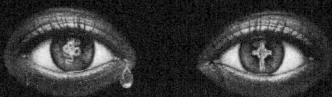

CHAPTER 16

> "

Beware that, when fighting monsters, you yourself do not become a monster... for when you gaze long into the abyss. The abyss gazes also into you.

FRIEDRICH W. NIETZSCHE

f there is a pain more devastating than the death of your mother, I never want to experience it.

I spent hours replaying our life together in my mind, and could not isolate a single moment or experience, even bad ones, I would want to go back and change. I wasn't so earnest that I considered my relationship with my mother perfect. But she was always, enough. She gave me all she had, even when she lacked so much mentally and emotionally because of the way my dad treated her. It didn't help that she and I had gotten closer in the years following his death.

I don't know if anything will ever fill this cavernous void.

I was disappointed Alicen wasn't with me. When she told me she wanted to hang back and let me be with my "family" all I could think was, **"YOU are my family too."** But I was dealing with so much at the time, I didn't have the strength to push the issue. It broke my heart she didn't insist on coming when she saw how much my mom's death affected me. Sadly, I was getting used to her being "unavailable" when I needed her most. I'm no psychologist or marriage counselor, but I was sure that was not something a husband (or wife) should learn to accept.

I made a mental note, packed my bag, and let it go.

The mood at my mother's memorial was somber. I was surrounded by a small gathering of family and a few old friends. Time passed slowly but it felt good to slow down, despite the circumstances.

I watched my aunt and Lance talk to each other as if they had known one another for years. She reminded me so much of my mom. Funny, loving, selfless. The women in my life were amazing.

During the brief memorial, as the Pastor delivered the eulogy, I reflected on the woman who had shaped my life in ways I could only begin to comprehend. Mom's passing had left a void in my heart, one that seemed impossible to fill.

The modest ceremony, planned according to her final wishes, was a testament to her simplicity and grace. She had made all the arrangements, right down to choosing the urn. My mom had somehow found an artist to hand paint an image of me and my brother on the simple vase, her final resting place.

It was a stark contrast to the turmoil and pain she had endured silently during her illness, a burden she had chosen not to share with anyone, not even her own sons.

My aunt's revelation about Mom's meticulous preparation for her memorial didn't surprise me. It was typical of her to think of others even in her final moments, sparing us the additional burden of making arrangements while we grieved. She even made sure my aunt could stay in the house.

They worked hard in the short time they had with one another to make up for lost time. My mom would tell me stories of their "sister dates," and the long talks they would have over coffee at brunch.

It made me feel good knowing she and Lance were not alone.

I exchanged memories and caught up with old friends from high school. I hadn't seen them since I left for the Navy. My mom had been like a surrogate mother to these guys, having them over for dinner after football games and tutoring them in math so they wouldn't fail and get dropped from the team. Man, I hadn't thought about that stuff in years. Now that I knew how much my mother was holding in, the fact she found enough compassion to help a group of guys survive the awkward challenges of high school made me admire her even more.

We talked about her famous meatloaf, and the time she caught us sneaking my father's beer out of the refrigerator. She promised not to tell him, but we had to pass the next math test with an 80 or more.

Good times.

I was grateful they came. Their unexpected show of support was just what I needed.

We paid our respects and said our farewells. I braced myself for the task ahead – the responsibility of fulfilling Mom's final wishes for Lance. In a couple of days, he would be accompanying our aunt on the long drive to Chicago. I finalized the itinerary with her and spent the rest of the time with my brother.

I felt a little guilty; after all these years, I couldn't shake the feeling I had turned my back on him and my mom trying to escape my father and the heavy-handed way he ran our lives.

I asked Lance how he was feeling, and he turned away. Maybe he was thinking the same thing I was afraid everyone thought... "Why do you care? You left us."

I couldn't shake off the weight of the responsibilities now resting on my shoulders. I watched Lance's solemn expression, sensing his sadness mingled with confusion, and I assured him I would never turn my back on him again, and promised we'd spend more time with each other when he came to live with us in Chicago. I told him that Alicen was really excited about him coming. The mention of her name got a response; his eyes widened and he smiled. I was so happy he loved Alicen. That would make the transition so much easier.

With a heavy heart but a newfound sense of purpose, I left Kentucky behind, again, knowing that the road ahead would be fraught with challenges, but determined to honor Mom's memory every step of the way.

5:42 A.M.

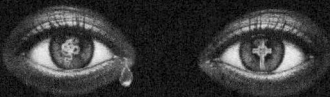

CHAPTER 17

66

'Tis better to have loved and lost, than never to have loved at all.

ALFRED LORD TENNYSON

W hen I got home, I sensed some awkwardness in Alicen's demeanor. Something felt off. **The vibe was really uncomfortable.**

"Hey," I began, breaking the silence. "Did you guys find out anything?"

She seemed ready to burst with the news.

"Oh my God, yes! Not only is Caitlyn not Haitian, but she's also half-white."

My eyes widened in disbelief. "Are you serious?"

"Yes! We met her biological mother, and let me tell you, the stories..."

Alicen trailed off, leaving me intrigued.

"What about her father?" I asked, curiosity getting the best of me.

Alicen shrugged. "All her mom would tell us is that he was married and took exceptionally good care of her financially. That was their agreement for her silence."

"Why did she place Caitlyn up for adoption?"

"She wanted her to have a balanced home life and upbringing, but she couldn't provide that herself," Alicen explained.

"Oh, wow..." I muttered, overwhelmed by the unexpected revelations. "I don't even know what to say."

As we unloaded the car, Alicen seemed to change the subject abruptly, shifting the conversation to a topic that had been discussed at length before.

"So, anyway... about your brother living with us..." she began, her tone carrying a hint of uncertainty.

A wave of suspicion washed over me, sensing a shift in her demeanor. "Is there a problem?" I asked, my voice tinged with caution.

"Well, actually, there is," she confessed, her words hanging in the air with an underlying tension. **"I'm not comfortable with Lance living here. You're away so often, and we're alone. I don't feel safe."**

Confusion mingled with frustration inside me. We had discussed this exhaustively, arriving at a mutual understanding. The weight of recent events, the loss of my mother, had already been taxing, and now the woman I loved seemed to be changing her stance.

"We talked about this, Ali," I replied, my voice betraying disbelief and frustration.

"No," she contradicted, her tone cool and distant. "I wanted to discuss it, but we never revisited the topic."

I felt my patience waning, my emotions raw and exposed. The constant shifting of Alicen's stance, her callousness, and her dismissiveness were wearing me down, especially in the wake of my mother's passing. I couldn't fathom how she could be so indifferent to the struggles I was going through.

"**What's the problem, then?**" I asked, my voice laced with a mixture of frustration and weariness.

She hesitated, as if contemplating her words carefully.

"**One time, while we were there visiting your mom,**" she began, her voice softer, "**he walked in on me in the shower.**"

The shock of her revelation jolted me, nearly causing me to drop the suitcase I held tightly. I couldn't fathom the magnitude of such an intrusion and violation.

"What?" I stammered, my voice trembling with a blend of anger and disbelief.

"**He ripped the shower curtain open and tried to force himself on me,**" Alicen confessed, her words hanging heavy in the air.

She shook her head, her eyes haunted by the memories. "Your mom heard me scream and came to my rescue. I was left crying, nervous, and afraid... a yo-yo of emotions." Her voice quivered with the weight of the past. "Your mom and I had a long talk about it, and she made me promise never to tell you. She didn't want you to be hurt by the truth about your brother."

The world around me seemed to spin, the floor beneath me unsteady. I struggled to comprehend the depth of the betrayal and the extent of the secrets people kept from me.

"Can this situation get any worse?" I muttered, trapped in a web of conflicting emotions and shattered trust.

"I'm sorry I never told you," Alicen whispered, her voice filled with remorse. "But I never thought I would have to face this decision."

My mind raced, torn between my promise to my mother and the present reality. I felt the weight of an impossible choice pressing down on me. No matter my decision, there would be consequences that could forever alter my life.

"We have a 24-hour care facility building at work," Alicen suggested, attempting to find a compromise. "He could stay there, and I would be able to keep an eye on him. It's the closest we can get to having him with us without compromising our safety."

The idea gave me a glimmer of hope, a potential solution to a seemingly insurmountable problem. "I suppose that wouldn't be so bad," I reluctantly admitted, acknowledging the practicality of the arrangement. With heavy hearts, we agreed that this would be the plan moving forward, searching for a fragile sense of stability in the midst of chaos.

With the decision made, life gradually regained a semblance of normalcy. The constant strain between Alicen and me seemed to ease as we found a compromise regarding my brother's living situation.

One weekend, I visited my brother at the care facility. As I walked through the doors, I found him sitting in a common area, a slight sadness in his eyes. He seemed glad to see me. However, he always wanted me to stay longer each time I visited.

I took solace in the fact he appeared clean and well taken care of. The staff at the facility seemed dedicated to his well-being, providing the support he needed. If he couldn't be home with me, this was the next best thing.

Some days, I felt something was not right.

Deep down, I knew my brother was still mourning, just as I was. My mother had been his only real caretaker, and her absence must weigh heavily on him. I wished I could have done more, been there for him like my mother.

The loss of our mother had hit him hard, harder than I could have ever imagined. As we sat together in silence, he suddenly turned to me somberly and said, "I miss Mom. I wish I could be with her."

My heart clenched. I struggled to find the right words. When I gently told him that Mom was gone, that she was dead, his response sent a chill down my spine. "I know," he whispered, his voice barely audible. **"I want to be dead too, to be with her."**

Confusion clouded my mind. I grappled with the realization that my brother, despite his autism, was contemplating suicide. I had always believed that people with mental challenges like his were somehow immune to such thoughts.

When the doctors came in for their usual rounds, I stepped out into the waiting room. While I waited for them to finish talking with Lance, I purchased a Snickers bar from the vending machine, took out my cell phone, and Googled "What is the correlation between autism spectrum disorder (ASD) and suicidal thoughts or behaviors?"

I learned It had been a topic of growing interest but remained somewhat limited. Some studies suggested that individuals with ASD may be at increased risk for suicidal ideation and attempts compared to the general population because social difficulties and challenges with communication, common characteristics of ASD, can lead to feelings of isolation and loneliness. These are known risk factors for suicidal thoughts. Additionally, co-occurring mental health conditions such as depression and anxiety, which are more prevalent in individuals with ASD, can also contribute to an increased risk of suicidal ideation.

I consulted with the doctor briefly and asked him if I should be concerned about what my brother shared. He reassured me that, based on his interaction with Lance, there were no signs of depression, and certainly no indication he wanted to harm himself.

I wasn't satisfied with his answer but didn't press him. He rushed off to his next patient and I stepped back into the room and sat beside Lance.

I'm not sure what that doctor was seeing, but the person I was looking at was defeated, sad, despondent. I did my best to console him and tried to change the subject. The more I talked, the further away he seemed to drift.

Later that evening, I told Alicen what Lance said. She listened with a grave expression. **"This is serious," she said, her voice tinged with concern. "We need to keep a close eye on him, make sure he gets the help he needs."** Her words echoed in my mind as I thought about the possibility of losing my brother, too. I had already endured the pain of losing our mother; I couldn't bear the thought of losing him as well.

The days passed, and we found a rhythm. The upcoming campaign brought a welcomed distraction, a flurry of activity that momentarily pushed the pain to the periphery. Though still tinged with a lingering emptiness, the house began to feel like a home once again. We tried our best to focus on moving forward.

As we settled into a routine, life took an unexpected turn, shattering any remaining fragments of stability we had managed to piece together.

We got the call at 5:42 a.m.

My brother tragically took his own life within the confines of the care facility. The physician on call said he had been battling depression. That night, he was overcome by an overwhelming sense of misery and despair. They sedated him and had planned on calling me the next day to discuss mental care options. He hung himself while the attendant on duty had stepped away for a cigarette break.

An agonizing realization settled in my spirit. I should have seen this coming. The signs were there, hidden in my consciousness, but I chose to ignore them. I let my desperation cloud my judgment and blind me to potential consequences. Alicen had made it abundantly clear that it was either this arrangement or nothing. I convinced myself this was the only solution, the only way to balance honoring my mother's wishes and saving my marriage.

The weight of guilt pressed down with unbearable force. I had betrayed my mother's memory for a woman who had become so cavalier about our marriage, about my brother's well-being.

A hatred I never felt began bubbling inside me. I resented Alicen for her lack of understanding and her failure to recognize the severity of the situation. I left him in her care. How could she not see this coming? She had chosen convenience over compassion, opting to confine my brother to an institution rather than seek the help he needed.

I looked at the wreckage of our lives, regretting the path we had chosen. The guilt, the sorrow, and the unfathomable loss were all a testament to the fact that actions have consequences.

Hate swirled within me like a tempest. I could only pray to find a way to heal, to salvage what remained of our shattered lives.

"Martin, I am so sorry," she managed to say, her voice heavy with the weight of her own grief.

"I don't know how this could have happened."

I glared at her and spit out the only words I could manage…

"Well, it did."

There was nothing left to say, no solace in the silence that enveloped us.

TALKING POINTS

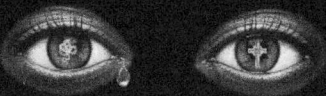

CHAPTER 18

"

If evil is spoken of you and it be true, correct yourself, if it be a lie, laugh at it.

EPICTETUS

Two long, agonizing months slipped by, marked by the aftermath of that devastating nightmare. We had just found our groove again, seeing flashes of the love we once shared. I swear, these days, all I could think was, if it's not one bad thing, it's another.

"Something's gotta give," I would say to myself, sometimes several times a day.

Ali found it difficult to return to her job. I wasn't surprised. The trauma of the rape left an indelible mark on her, fracturing her sense of security and trust. The thought of returning to the scene where the unimaginable had happened filled her with dread. I felt awful. This used to be where she was at her best, doing the work she had always dreamed about. She would come home and talk about how she felt she was making a difference in so many lives.

Now, the only thing different…was her.

One morning, the situation went from horrible to dreadful. Ali found out she was pregnant. My wife was carrying her rapist's baby. Her refusal to press charges against her attacker outweighed the sheer scale of that earth-shattering news.

We argued about it for weeks, and she would not give in.

"I am just having a really hard time understanding how you can let this guy get away with violating you, Alicen."

She let out a guttural, "ugh!", to let me know she was tired of hearing me talk about it.

"You can be pissed all you want, but I'm your husband. I am the one who has to see you in pain, listen to you cry in your sleep. I wasn't there to protect you Alicen, that is bad enough. Now, you won't even let me do the one thing that would give me some consolation."

"Marty, how many times do I have to explain?"

"Clearly, as many times as it will take to make me understand why we are not prosecuting this animal to the fullest extent of the law!" I yelled.

"The man is mentally challenged!" she shot back. "Jesus, he was completely confused, Martin. He mistook my caring and my kindness for some twisted sense of love. He didn't know what he was doing! How can I send a sick man to jail?"

"I don't know. By filing charges."

I was done walking on eggshells. She ignored the sarcasm.

"In his mind, I was his wife," she reasoned. "The intricacies of the human mind, Martin, they're complex. But I don't expect you to understand."

"You know what I understand? In *real* life, you are *my* wife. But that doesn't seem to mean a damn thing to you anymore, Alicen. Fuck whatever I feel. You are just going to do whatever you want."

She brought her knees to her chest and buried her face between them.

No matter how hard I struggled to reconcile my anger and thirst for justice with the depth of Ali's compassion, my internal conflict simmered.

"So, how are we going to handle this pregnancy?" I asked, bracing myself for more pushback. "Can we at least agree on a solution to that?"

The thought that a life was growing within her, conceived in the darkest of moments, seared my soul.

"I'd been doing some research. Statistics showed approximately 50% of rape-related pregnancies end in abortion."

Leave it to my wife to be on the wrong end of the data. But behind those numbers, I knew that the choice ultimately belonged to Alicen.

"Well...no answer?" I asked.

"About what?" she snapped.

"The baby," I replied.

"What do you mean?"

"You can't possibly be considering carrying to full term?" I fumed.

"Are you suggesting I terminate it?" She asked. "I know Mr. Pro-Life is not talking about abortion."

"Don't play games with me, Alicen. You know damn well this is not the same!"

"I can't believe you, Martin. You're on TV, at rallies, and town hall meetings, talking all of this pro-life crap, yet here you are, using the A-word."

"Your point?"

"Do you guys believe any of the words y'all tell those cameras and crowds or are they just talking points?" she asked.

I was not backing down.

"So, let me get this straight. You are really sitting there, basking in your audacity, trying to convince me I have no right to care that my wife is not only considering carrying her rapist's baby to term, but she may want to raise it?"

"The only audacious person in this room right now is you, Martin. I will never for the life of me figure out how you make everything about you."!

"Man, if that is not the pot…"

I caught myself. The hatred I saw in her eyes stopped me cold.

"Say it, Martin. Say it!"

"Now who is trying to twist the topic to make it about them?"

I could feel the heat of anger radiating from her body.

"Everything, everything we have talked about, that mattered, just a bunch of lies," she sputtered.

I stared at her, and didn't blink, knowing how much she hated that.

"Well, I know the pro-life stance was bullshit. What else was a bunch of smoke and mirrors? Veteran's rights? Have you forgotten how badly veterans are treated, Sailor?"

"Where are you going with this, Alicen?"

"I'm just saying. I've yet to hear you talk about that in an interview. It used to infuriate you, seeing how the government treated our vets. You'd come back from the VA, trembling because you saw firsthand how badly people talked to them. You told me how long they had to wait to be seen by a doctor and how hard it was to make a simple mental health appointment?

I refused to be re-routed.

"Are you having this baby?"

"I held you when you cried after hearing how many veterans were committing suicide because they felt alone, unloved, discarded. Yet, I can't remember a single debate where that was a priority."

"Are. You. Keeping. This. Baby?"

"And now, President ass-clown is literally rallying crowds with border wall talk. We spent hours talking about how horribly immigrants were being treated in this country!"

"Alicen..."

"You and Caitlyn, sitting in our living room, talking about DACA, and TPS, and the terrible way those policies were handled."

"You are pushing it Alicen."

"Wasn't it your precious President Reagan that said, 'We should tear down walls'? What, that doesn't fit your new agenda, Martin? When did the mission change for the party?"

"Alicen..."

"What?" she snapped.

"I am tired of the hypocrisy, Martin. How could you stand next to any of those guys? How do you stomach the way they talk about the LGBTQ community? Do you ever think how bad that's hurting your aunt?"

She definitely had these verbal guns loaded for a while, and she was unloading an entire vitriolic clip into my chest. I knew I should stop her before she said something she could never take back. Before both of us did. But she was raging, and I was tired.

She was on a roll.

"For a guy who hated the ways of your father, you are becoming him. The apple did not fall far from that evil tree."

There it was. I had no reply.

She stomped into the bedroom. I heard her cell phone ring. She answered.

"Seriously...now?" I muttered. This woman is unbelievable.

I could hear her talking to someone. Probably Caitlyn. There wasn't much she didn't tell her.

Out of nowhere, I heard, "No way!"

Alicen rushed out of the bedroom.

"What now?" I asked. "You want to tell me more about how much you hate me?"

"Did you ever check your DNA results?" She asked.

"I don't give a..."

She cut me off before I could finish and handed me the phone.

"Caitlyn wants to talk to you."

I rolled my eyes and reluctantly took the phone.

"Hey, Caitlyn, look now is not a good...?

The sound of her sobbing stopped me cold.

"Martin," she said, heaving. Do you remember someone named Elnora? She used to work for your parents?"

"Several people worked for my parents. I don't remember all of their names. Why?"

She sniffed, and after a few seconds, said, "This would have been when you were around four or five years old."

"Yeah," I said, the memory started to come back. "There was a lady and I think that was her name. Why do you ask? Why are you crying?"

"We're siblings, Martin," Caitlyn sputtered.

"What?" I was confused. "How the hell did we get here?"

"Your father is my biological father."

Alicen must have convinced this woman to make up a story so outlandish, it would take my mind off the argument we'd been having.

"That is so not possible, Caitlyn. I don't know where you are getting this from, but you're wrong."

"Please check your DNA results, Martin. Let me know what you find." I handed the phone back to Alicen, at a loss for words.

"I'll call you back, girl. Take deep breaths and try to calm down, please."

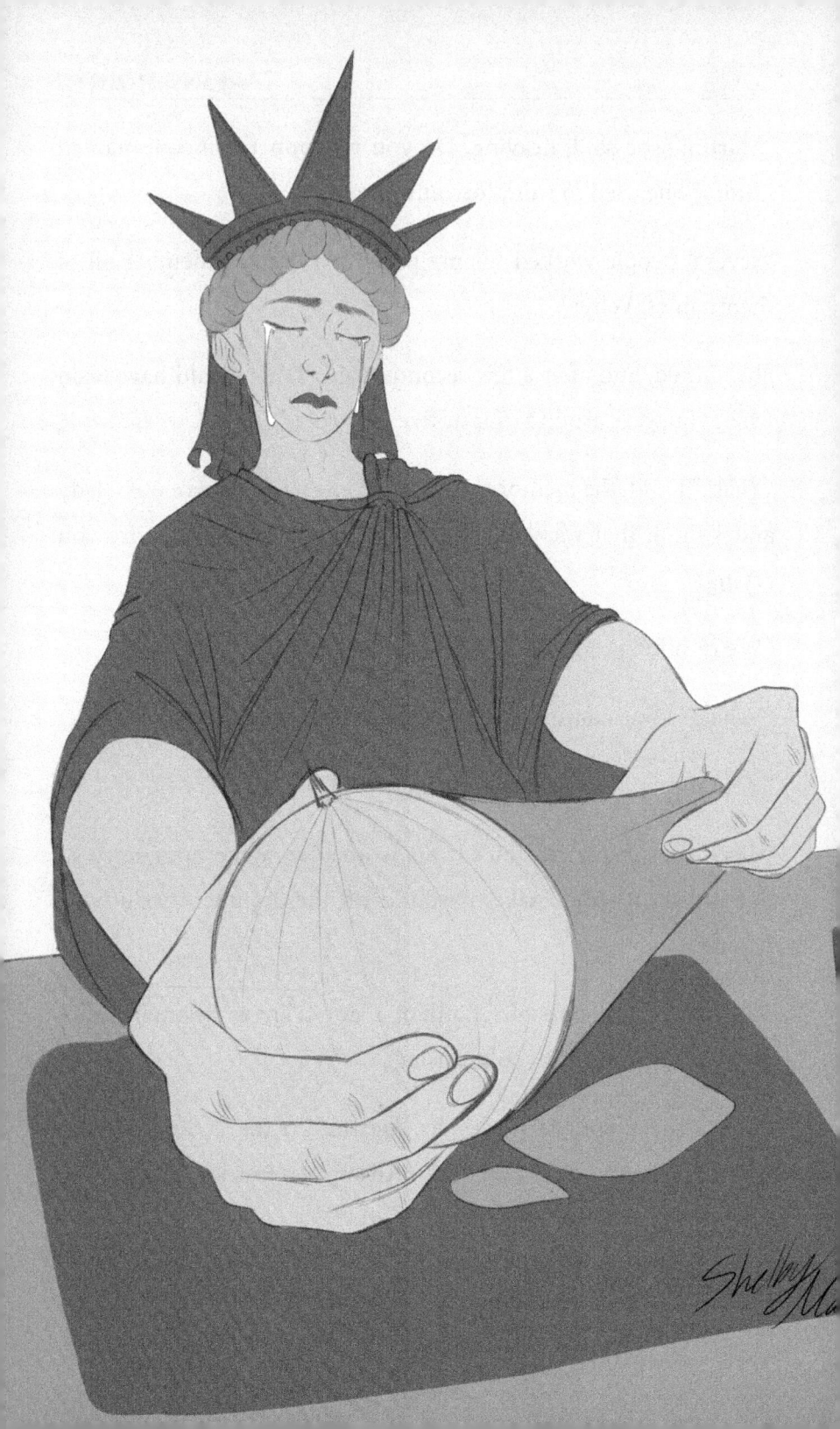

more shocking, Martin? That your dad cheated or that your sister is black?"

"My father despised black people. This can't be. I don't understand."

She took a deep breath, and shook her head slowly, as if she could not believe I could be so stupid.

"Martin, this type of thing has been going on longer than America cares to acknowledge. Here we go again with the damn hypocrisy!"

"You know what, Alicen…shut up. Just shut up! I'm sick of your self-righteous, entitled attitude!"

She cocked her head to the side, raised one eyebrow, and twisted her lips. I knew this was her getting wound up, and I was ready to give it right back to her.

"Bro, you have been around your Republican buddies for way too long. Caitlyn was right about you. You ain't nothing but another good ol' white boy. I didn't believe it, no matter how many people tried to warn me. They said one day you would show your entire ass. I guess that day is here."

"Alicen, I don't know who you think you are right now, but you need to walk away before this entire conversation goes completely left."

"Don't threaten me."

"Oh, it's not a threat. It's a promise. You have insulted me, disrespected me, and tried to emasculate me, all because I wanted you to make a decision, one time, that put us first, instead of your own needs."

"Whatever Martin."

"And then you hit me with the low blow of saying I am just like my father?"

"Yep, selfish, hypocritical, hateful, entitled. Just. Like. Him."

"Well damn, I don't know if I am exactly like him, but I am really beginning to see why he felt the way he did about you people!"

The words came out before I could catch them. The final nail in a coffin filled with the remnants of our relationship. Whatever we had was gone. Not even on life support. Flatlined.

"*You people!*" Alicen echoed my words, looking like she was about to choke. Tears welled in her eyes.

"The truth...finally."

She ran back into the bedroom. I followed close behind and arrived just in time to see her pull out a suitcase and start packing.

"Where are you going, Alicen?"

"Don't even worry about it. You are free to go find a pasty, blonde-haired, blue-eyed, busted-down version of me to spend the rest of your life with. I'm done with this shit, you son of a bitch."

In my wildest dreams, on the craziest day, I would have never believed we would end this way.

She headed toward the door and turned the knob. Before stepping out of my life, she turned slowly. Her eyes narrowed, her nose flared, and her voice was hoarse from crying and yelling.

"Before I go, Martin, I want to ask you a question."

I looked into her eyes, wondering what more could be left to say.

"What bothers you more? The fact that this child growing inside me is not yours, or the fact that it is *black?*"

"Alicen," I stared, "you can't be serious."

"Very," she snarled.

When I didn't respond, she scoffed.

"Just as I thought."

She stormed out.

Minutes later, I walked toward the bedroom. Before crossing the threshold toward the bed I once shared with the love of my life, I let out a primal growl and punched the wall so hard the vase on the adjoining table fell to the floor.

Like the life I used to know, it shattered into a million pieces.

THE ULTIMATUM

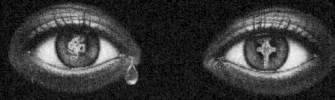

CHAPTER 19

"

We all know that Art is not truth. Art is a lie that makes us realize the truth, at least the truth that is given to us to understand.

PABLO PICASSO

The scent of Angel, Alicen's favorite perfume, lingered in the air, a ghost of her presence after our fight. It's funny how something as simple as a fragrance could stir up memories. For years, every time I inhaled her neck deeply, the smell of her perfume ignited my passion, made me feel safe. After tonight, I'm sure if I even sense a hint of that perfume in the air, I will get physically ill.

The stark silence echoed the emptiness I felt inside. My heartbeat hammered against my ribs, a counterpoint to the chilling quiet.

I started to reflect on the final moments of the last hour, and my mind drifted back to the three minutes before Alicen breezed past me, bags in hand, and slammed the door behind her. I remember standing frozen, a silent observer listening to the heated exchange taking place in the bedroom. Alicen's voice, sharp with hurt, reached me like a distant storm, distorted by the cracks in our relationship. I strained to catch every syllable, desperate to decipher the cryptic messages hidden within her tirade.

"I can't believe you're saying this, Caitlyn," her voice raw and intense, the emotional release resonating deeply. "After everything..."

Her voice cracked.

I started to walk out of the apartment into the hallway, feeling guilty that I was privy to this awful argument between best friends. But I was too invested at this point, and I wanted to see how it ended.

Alicen's words hung heavy, weighed down by unspoken accusations and unresolved pain. The tension thickened the air until it almost suffocated me. The realization that Caitlyn was on the other end sent a wave of anxiety crashing over me.

"I trusted you, Caitlyn," Alicen's voice trembled, a volatile mix of betrayal and anger lacing her tone. "Now... I don't know what to believe anymore. How could you do this to me?"

I stood rooted; my heartbeat drummed against my ribs as their conversation washed over me in waves of conflicting emotions. Every fiber of my being wanted to intervene, but I remained trapped, my curiosity morbid and manipulative.

"What the hell is this about?" I whispered, my inner monologue spouting furiously as I tried to decipher the situation.

"She's raging tonight," I said to myself. My thoughts spiraled, searching for meaning, trying to understand why Caitlyn was catching a stray.

"You have to choose, Caitlyn," Alicen's voice sliced through the air, sharp and unforgiving. "It's him or me... and you better make the right choice."

The weight of her ultimatum settled on my shoulders. She was attacking the people closest to her one by one, pushing us away, unleashing a barrage of hurtful words intended to cut deep. Her words echoed in the empty spaces, stark reminders of the distance that had grown between us.

Then, with a finality that even left me reeling, the call ended.

The stifling silence of our argument, the weight of the overheard conversation, it all pressed down on me. I was standing amidst the wreckage of shattered dreams, grappling with the painful truth of love falling apart.

As I sat in the living room, the emotional rollercoaster of the day still churning within me, a knock at the door jolted me from my thoughts. With a sigh, I dragged myself to the door. It flew open before I could reach for the doorknob. Caitlyn strolled in, cautiously, the familiar sight of her face offering a strange mix of comfort and unease.

"Hey," she said softly, her expression a reflection of concern and something deeper, something unspoken. "I let myself in."

I almost laughed out loud at her admission. She always let herself in. She did the same thing when we were in the dorms. Alicen and I would be sitting on the couch, watching a movie, and she'd bust through the door already dramatically, already in full-on storytelling mode. This was not a new occurrence.

Clearly, we were all on edge, treading lightly, afraid to cause more damage by saying or doing the wrong thing.

At this rate, none of us was sure if life could get any worse.

I hesitated, the silence stretching.

"What are you doing here?" My voice was rough, laced with exhaustion. "This... this isn't a good time."

Caitlyn's gaze swept across the room, lingering on the empty spaces that harkened back to happier times.

She took a deep breath, her words measured yet heavy with emotion.

"Actually," she started, her voice hesitant, "I was trying to catch up with Alicen. But it looks like she's not here."

My heart jumped at the mention of Alicen's name, the memory of our fight fresh and gut-wrenching. Despite my turmoil, curiosity gnawed at me, forcing the inevitable question.

"She left. Pissed. I heard you two arguing but could only make out her side of the conversation."

She hung her head down, avoiding eye contact. I was not used to this timid version of a woman who, for years, carried herself like Haitian royalty, confident and regal. It was jarring.

I continued to press her.

"What were you two talking about?" I asked.

Caitlyn's expression darkened.

"We… we were fighting," she admitted, her voice barely above a whisper. "About us."

"Us?" I echoed, confusion swirling in my mind.

"Yeah," she confirmed with a sigh. "Me and you. About us being related. About you being my brother."

"I heard her tell you to choose. Choose what?" I interrogated.

"Choose between you... and her," she admitted sheepishly.

I was floored.

"I... I didn't know what to expect," Caitlyn continued, her voice trembling slightly. "Part of me was... was hopeful, you know? Hoping that maybe we could... could build something, finally get to know each other."

My head was spinning. I listened in stunned silence, the weight of Caitlyn's words sinking in. But my thoughts were interrupted as Caitlyn recounted Alicen's response, her voice tinged with hurt and frustration.

"But Alicen... she wasn't having it," Caitlyn admitted, her voice breaking slightly. "She said that our friendship should be stronger than... than some relationship we never knew existed. She told me to choose between you and her."

A heavy silence hung in the air as I processed Caitlyn's words, grappling with the magnitude of the situation. The bond we shared with Caitlyn had become a source of comfort and stability as our friendship matured. Now it wavered on the edge of uncertainty.

"I told her... I told her I wanted to get to know my brother," Caitlyn confessed, her voice wavering with emotion.

"I take it she didn't take that well," I said facetiously.

"Obviously, Marty. She was gutted that someone she loved, someone she trusted, pretty much told her that another person was more important to them than she was."

I could not imagine how much that hurt; to hear your best friend tell you that, in the grand scheme of things, you don't measure up. I imagined Alicen questioning if she was ever really important to Caitlyn; if their bond was as strong as she thought all these years.

As angry as I was at how Alicen behaved earlier, I felt for her.

"How did you guys leave it?" I asked as if I didn't know.

"She... she told me to go to hell and hung up."

A pang of sadness mingled with the tangled mess of emotions swirling inside me. It became painfully clear that our world was shifting in ways we had never imagined. I looked at this woman, my newly discovered sister, ironically the closest relative I had, and did not have a clue what to do. Should I console her? Did I owe her that? I had my own problems right now and didn't have the mental or emotional strength to carry someone else's mess.

But she wasn't just "someone." She and I shared the same bloodline, the same legacy.

And right now, she was all I had.

As I grappled with the weight of our newfound connection, I wondered what the future held for us all.

FORBIDDEN UNION

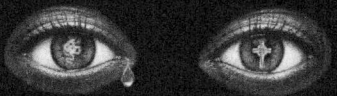

CHAPTER 20

"

I seek truth over a lie; I seek justice over injustice; I seek righteousness over the rewards of evildoers, and I love Allah more than I love the state.

H. RAP BROWN

They say whenever we make plans, God laughs. Well, I don't know who "they" are, but I wonder if the same people also say that as soon as you think your life is going perfectly, God really cracks up!

Days after my entire world came crashing down, I finally came up for air. In my darkest hour, my campaign manager proved his worth. **During my unplanned hiatus, he surpassed every expectation and earned every penny of his salary.** The guy kept the momentum of my political aspirations going as I struggled under the weight of a truth I never saw coming.

Caitlyn, a woman who despised me for years, was my sister. How could this be?

My father was a bona fide racist. **He preached hate as effortlessly as he breathed.** Yet, this man's mind was so twisted he **betrayed his own sickening beliefs by having an affair with a Black woman.**

Elnora, of all people. She was once practically part of the family. My mother relied on this woman when caring for my brother began taking a toll on her mentally and physically.

Honestly, I was pretty pissed at Elnora, too. She was complicit in the betrayal. A willing participant in their disturbing entanglement. Lord knows, my mother didn't deserve it. I was relieved she was dead. I would have been gutted if I had to watch her struggle with this revelation.

Now, I have to deal with the aftermath and the consequences of their depravity. Caitlyn. My sister. **The product of their forbidden union.**

The weight of this knowledge bore down on me. Mom and Lance, gone. Alicen, gone.

Now, I was facing the prospect of losing my sister. I couldn't believe I was even saying the words. Sister. I have a sister.

I couldn't lose any more family. I had to find a way to let go of the past.I summoned the nerve to call Caitlyn. She was surprisingly open when I invited her to meet at a local coffee shop.

Sitting in a dimly lit corner, sipping cappuccinos, Caitlyn and I opened up about our anger, resentment, and fears. We talked for hours. We clearly had more to work through when we left the coffee shop.

We walked to a nearby park and found a bench under a streetlight. We were both pretty distraught but still had the presence of mind to be careful. It was still Chicago.

Hours passed, and we unwittingly began forging a sibling attachment. Amid the chaos, we found a safe space.

"Marty, I'm scared. I'm scared of what this means for us, for our families. I don't even know who I am anymore!"

Caitlyn was grappling with some deep issues in the wake of the truth. The family that raised her was never meant to be permanent guardians. They had kidnapped her. They literally stole her from her birth mother after she left Catilyn in their care while she got her life together.

All her life, no matter how hard things got, she clung to the fierce pride and power that came with being the daughter of Haitian immigrants. Her history was her anchor, her fuel, her fire!

Now, she was adrift. She questioned everything she knew about herself and where she truly belonged.

She sighed heavily and said, "I never expected that reality would bring so much confusion and doubt into my life."

I felt bad for her.

"I understand, Caitlyn. I've been feeling the same way. This complete disaster turned everything upside down. I don't think Alicen is ever coming back."

Caitlyn's eyes widened in surprise.

"Really? Alicen wants to leave you? I didn't realize things were *that* bad."

I nodded slowly.

"Yeah, she's been questioning our relationship for a long time. I want to save our marriage and prove that I'm willing to change and grow, but she's not having it."

"Dam, Marty. **She had mentioned she felt you weren't the man she married**, but I just thought it was normal husband and wife stuff."

"Have you spoken to her?" I asked cautiously. Her silence let me know she had and the conversation had not gone well.

"She accused me of turning against her because I wanted to talk to you."

I was stunned. I thought Caitlyn's decision to talk to me was admirable. She could've told me to go to hell and put all this behind her. I respected her courage. I did not know Alicen saw it as some kind of betrayal.

"I don't get it," Caitlyn said, fighting back tears. "We have been through so much together. We confided in each other, supported each other."

I knew all this to be true! Their friendship weathered storms that very few people knew about.

I guess Alicen felt like Caitlyn choosing to prioritize her connection with me meant she was abandoning everything they had built.

"You would think that she, of all people, would understand," she said, burying her face in her hands. "She knows me better than anyone! I would never do anything to hurt her. How could she not understand why you and I had to talk?"

"How did you guys leave it"? I asked, trying not to sound self-serving. I knew Caitlyn was my only connection to Alicen. If I had a chance to reconcile with her, it would have to start with the woman sitting across from me.

But right now, it wasn't about me.

"I told her that discovering the truth about my origins, about you being my brother, shook me to my core, and I had to address it, or I'd lose my mind."

"Let me guess, she said you were selfish."

"Yep. Even after I begged her to see it from my perspective. I wanted to find out who I am, where I come from, and that didn't mean I was rejecting everything we shared."

I took a deep breath and said with determination, "I want to make it work, Caitlyn. I want to break free from the cycle of hurt. We need to take the time to understand who we are as individuals; embrace the complexities of our past."

From that day on, we talked for hours on end. Days blended into nights. We dissected the signs we missed, the missing pieces of our lives we never thought to question. Because of these conversations, we discovered the depths of our mutual experiences. We were victims of our father's choices.

On a brighter note, we also shared a love for art, a passion for social justice, and an affinity for adventure.

Our kinship, new and still confusing at times, was being built on trust, empathy, and a desire to heal. Conversations became a lifeline. Our shared DNA couldn't erase the fact that our father was a racist who had caused immense pain and suffering.

But we challenged those stereotypes and rose above the limitations that society placed upon us.

As we delved deeper into our past, **we discovered things about ourselves that we had long suppressed**, aspects of our identities that we needed to accept and work on. **Together, we confronted the racial stereotypes that had held us back.**

We were making progress when another revelation came crashing down on us. **Unfinished business loomed, threatening to change the trajectory of our new sibling relationship forever.**

DREAM SEQUENCE

"

There are only two things. Truth and lies. Truth is indivisible; hence it cannot recognize itself; anyone who wants to recognize it has to be a lie.

FRANZ KAFKA

M y heart pounded in my chest as my gaze locked with the figure before me. The dim light revealed the contours of his face. A mix of shock, denial, and reluctant acceptance washed over me.

"No... it can't be," I whispered, my voice barely audible over the relentless rush of water.

"Dad? How? Why?"

There was no escape. I was in the throes of a recurring nightmare triggered by Alicen's harsh words. She had gotten into my head. I didn't want to fall asleep tonight. I was so afraid I'd have another bad dream and come face to face with familiar demons.

I was caught in a disorienting haze, unsure of what was more terrifying—the realization that this was a nightmare or the inability to break free from its hold. Anxiety, fear, and an unwelcome reality swirled within my dreams, engulfing me, refusing to let me escape my truth. Alicen had awakened the dormant beast, the monster I had desperately tried to conceal deep within the recesses of my subconscious.

I couldn't have known that these demons would take the shape of my father.

His presence, once distant and elusive, now stood right in front of me, impossible to deny. Throughout my entire life, I had been running away from him—his beliefs, his toxicity, and the deep-rooted hatred he carried. I convinced myself that the farther I distanced myself from him, the less likely his influence would seep into my being. But now, as I confronted him in the depths of my subconscious, I couldn't ignore the truth that unfolded before me. His presence had left an undeniable impact on who I had become. Alicen called it. I was more like him than I wanted to admit.

I couldn't escape the similarities, the echoes of his actions and his words reflected in my life. The reality settled upon me, weighed me down, made it hard to breathe.

The sound of the water became deafening, no longer melodic or soothing. It was an enemy now, a reminder of our entrapment, of the danger that surrounded us.

I fought against the force of the rushing water, desperately trying to move toward the hatch. But my steps were impeded, hindered by the density of the flood. I was trapped in a chamber that was supposed to be secure and watertight, yet it was failing me when I needed it most.

My voice cracked with desperation as I called out to my father, begging for a plan, for a way out. But silence greeted me, amplifying the growing sense of hopelessness. He stood there, stoic and unmoving, unaffected by our dire circumstances.

"Why won't you answer me? We can't just stay here and die!" I shouted, frustration and fear distorting my voice. I reached out, *trying to grasp his arm in a desperate attempt to shake him out of his silence.*

He was unresponsive, his face an ominous mask in the dim light.

The water continued to rise, its relentless advance mirroring my mounting panic. Regrets flooded my mind. I thought about my loved ones, my unfinished dreams, and the person I could have become.

I couldn't tear my gaze away from my father. His features became more defined, and a chilling smile formed. It sent shivers down my spine, a sense of unease settling deep within me.

His voice, laced with disturbing satisfaction, finally broke the silence that enveloped us.

"Marty...son," he said, his words dripping with a dark undertone. "Did you really think you could escape me? I've always been here, part of you."

"I am nothing like you!"

The corners of his mouth curled up threateningly.

"Your wife saw right through you! Your reaction to finding out your sister is a Black woman? Priceless! It's always been in you, boy! You are your father's son!"

The laugh echoed about the cabin, maniacal, loud.

"Wake up, wake up, wake up," I willed myself.

"It won't matter, Marty. Whether you wake up or not, live or die, you will always be a Ruane. We are one and the same boy! You can't run from it!"

His laugh pierced my ears. I lunged at him. I intended to rip him apart! Annihilate him, as I'd wanted to do so many times growing up.

I felt a surge of cold dread coursing through my veins. The water rose higher, closing in on me, as his presence grew more ominous. His taunting laughter grew more intense. The sound of ringing rattled my brain.

Laughter. Ringing. Laughter. More ringing.

The sound grew persistent and loud enough to drown out my father's laughter. I was tired of him taunting me. I swung in his direction, ready to land what I prayed was a deadly plow. The momentum of my body sent me sailing off the bed. I hit the floor with a thud and sat up, disoriented.

The ringing had not stopped. I realized it was my phone. I rushed to answer before the caller hung up, hoping it was Alicen.

"Hello, hello…" I yelled desperately.

"Hi, Martin."

Why are you calling me?

"

Yesterday is not
ours to recover,
but tomorrow is
ours to win or lose.

LYNDON B. JOHNSON

THANK YOU SHELBY MACKELLAR AND CESAR GONZALEZ

I am incredibly proud of the artwork found throughout "Why Sell Lives When the Truth is Free." I understood, while writing the book, that the story had to be underscored by compelling, thought-provoking images intended to amplify the narrative's message, without overpowering the characters or their experiences.

The custom artwork herein is a labor of love brought to life by two exceptionally talented individuals.

Shelby MacKellar and Cesar Gonzalez were students of mine when I lectured at Lone Star College–University Park in Houston, Texas. It's hard to articulate how magical the entire process was, despite the simplicity with which the content was created! I would share my ideas for a chapter or a particular scene. Literally, I would plant a seed in their minds and pray they would grasp the concept, nurture it, and see it to its fruition.

Within days, Shelby, or Cesar, depending on which of the two had been assigned the design, would submit the artwork, capturing the essence of my vision to perfection.

I take immense pride in being their very first paying customer (a fact we joke about occasionally). It is with immeasurable gratitude I acknowledge that (and now others) recognize and support the remarkable talent they both possess.

It's safe to say that without their dedication and creative prowess, "Why Sell Lies When the Truth Is Free" wouldn't have come to life in such a deeply meaningful and touching way.

TO MY ESTEEMED PUBLISHER

To my esteemed publisher, Million Dollar Pen, Ink.,

I extend my heartfelt gratitude for the unwavering trust and steadfast support you have bestowed upon me and my creative vision. Throughout our enduring partnership, we have not only touched lives across the globe with the compelling narratives of my parents and grandparents in *"Life Is Not Complicated-YOU ARE"* but have also illuminated the path for those navigating the depths of darkness through *"The Other 99 T.Y.M.E.S: Train Your Mind to Enjoy Serenity."*

In this remarkable journey, you have provided me with the invaluable opportunity to craft what I humbly consider my most profound literary work to date. Your unyielding support and unwavering belief in my vision have served as both catalyst and elevation for my creativity, propelling it to heights I could have scarcely envisioned.

For these gifts, I am brimming with an immeasurable sense of gratitude. Our collaboration has been nothing short of transformative, and I eagerly anticipate the continued partnership as we embark on future literary endeavors.

With the deepest appreciation,

Carlos Wallace, Author

EVERY HERO DESERVES A PLAC

On October 31, 1967 Captain Riley Pitts made a heroi
service and personal sacrfice, along with the more than
danger of losing meaning to future generations. That is
right near this very spot, so the heroic deeds of those lik

LEARN HOW YOU CAN HEL

GEORGE
Founded a Nation.

THOMAS
Gave us the Constitution.

RE THEIR STORY IS TOLD.

service to our country. Riley's story of
es on the Vietnam Veterans Memorial is in
aising funds to build an Education Center,
ive amongst other great Americans.

uildTheCenter.org

ABRAHAM
Pr_____ed the Union

RILEY
At the cost of his life, went abov_
and beyond the call of duty.

BIO D LOSOYA · GEORGE WASHINGTON
TCHELL · ROBERT B. MOORE · WILLIS A
AC ROBINSON · THOMAS H. ROBERTS
ALSTON SUMMERLIN · WILLIAM E. S
H G WASHINGTON · THOMAS WATERS

Made in the USA
Columbia, SC
12 September 2025

61967422R00180